Ethical Wills

ETHICAL WILLS

A Modern Jewish Treasury

EDITED AND ANNOTATED BY

JACK RIEMER AND NATHANIEL STAMPFER

SCHOCKEN BOOKS
New York

First published by Schocken Books 1983
10 9 8 7 6 5 4 3 2 1   83   84   85   86

91-84

Library of Congress Cataloging in Publication Data
Main entry under title:
Ethical wills.
    Collection of wills originally written in English,
German, Hebrew, and Yiddish.
    1. Wills, Ethical—Collected works.   I. Riemer, Jack.
II. Stampfer, Nathaniel.
BJ1286.W59T65   1983   296.3'85   82—19160

Manufactured in the United States of America
Designed by Jacqueline Schuman
ISBN 0—8052—3839—5

Sholom Aleichem's will reprinted by permission of the Sholom Aleichem family. Epitaph translated by Bel Kaufman, Copyright © 1983 by Bel Kaufman and used with permission.

Avrohom Mordekhai Alter from *Emet-Ve-emuna* edited by Israel Ya'akov Arten, Jerusalem, 1948. Translated for this edition by Nathaniel Stampfer.

Amanut Publishing, Ltd.: Noam Grossman, from *Noam: Ner Neshama lezecher Noam Grossman shenafal he-hare yehuda,* Tel Aviv, 1948. Copyright © 1948 by Anna and Reuben Grossman. Translated for this edition by Nathaniel Stampfer.

American Jewish Archives: Benjamin M. Roth, "An Ethical Letter: Benjamin Roth to his Son, 1854," translated by Albert H. Friedlander in *American Jewish Archives,* Vol. VI, No. 1, 1954. Reprinted by permission of *American Jewish Archives.*

Joshua Chachik Publishing House, Ltd.: Shalom Ansky, Abba Berdiczew, Zippora Birman, Theodor Herzl, Edmond de Rothschild, Meir Dizengoff, Pinhas Rutenberg, Alter Ya'akov Sahrai, Moshe Sofer, Enzo Sereni, Hirsch Zaddok, Yitzhak Elhanan Spektor from *Sefer Hama'alot* edited by Eliezer Steinman, Tel Aviv, 1956. Copyright © 1956 by Joshua Chachik Publishing House, Ltd. Translated for this edition by Nathaniel Stampfer.

Crown Publishers: Avraham Kreizman, "For you I shall continue to live," translated by Eliezer Whartman, and Eldad Pan, "Life is worth little unless...," translated by Sidney Greenberg from *A Treasury of Comfort* edited by Sidney Greenberg, New York, 1954. Copyright © 1954 by Sidney Greenberg. Used by permission of Crown Publishers, Inc.

C.Y.C.O. Publishing House: A Mother's Will, A Polish Jew, Berl Tomshelski, Shulamit Rabinovitch, Shulamit Rabinovitch's Husband, On the Walls of Bialystok Prison from *Kiddush Hashem* edited by Sh. Niger, New York, 1948. Copyright © 1948 Louis LaMed Literary Foundation. Translated for this edition by Nathaniel Stampfer.

Abraham M. Ellis, *A Father's Counsel About the Paths of Life: The Ethical Will of Abraham M. Ellis.* Copyright © 1955 by Abraham M. Ellis. Reprinted by permission of Sidney M. Ellis.

Hamakrik Publishing, Ltd.: Elias Raphael Rosenbaum, "Testament of Elias Raphael Rosenbaum," translated by Mrs. Bertel Strauss, from *The Rosenbaums of Zell: A Study of a Family* by Berthold Strauss, London, 1962. Copyright © 1962 by Berthold Strauss.

Richard J. Israel, "In a Hospital Waiting Room" from *The Jewish Family Book* edited by Sharon Strassfeld and Kathy Green, New York, 1981, pp. 3 – 4. Reprinted by permission of Richard J. Israel.

Jewish Frontier Association: Hayim Greenberg from *Inner Eye: Selected Essays of Hayim Greenberg*, Vol. II, edited by Sholomo Katz. Copyright © 1964 by Jewish Frontier Publishing Association. Translated for this edition by Nathaniel Stampfer.

Jewish Historical Society of England: Gottlieb Wehle, "A Sabbathian Will from New York," by Gershom Scholem from *Miscellanies of the Jewish Historical Society of England: Essays in Memory of Elkan Nathan Adler,* Vol. V, 1948.

Yitzhak Kelman, from *Moreshet Avot,* edited by Rabbi Abraham Kelman, New York, 1974. Reprinted by permission of Wolfe Kelman. Translated for this edition by Jack Riemer.

Literistic, Ltd.: Sam Levenson, "Sam Levenson's Ethical Will and Testament to His Grandchildren and to Children Everywhere," from *Woman's Day,* May 3, 1977. Copyright © 1976 by Sam Levenson. Reprinted by permission of Literistic, Ltd.

Moment Magazine: Liebman Adler's will in "Two Ethical Wills" by Jack Riemer from *Moment,* Vol. 1, No. 1, May – June, 1975. Reprinted by permission of *Moment.*

Paulist Press: Abraham Isaac Kook from *Abraham Isaac Kook: The Essays of Penitence, Lights of Holiness, the Moral Principles, Essays, Letters and Poems,* translated by Rabbi Ben Zion Bokser. Copyright © 1978 by Ben Zion Bokser. Reprinted by permission of the Paulist Press.

Schocken Books Inc.: Hannah Senesh from *Hannah Senesh: Her Life and Diary,* New York, 1972, pp. 131 – 34. Copyright © 1966 by Hakibbutz Hameuchad Publishing House, Ltd.; Copyright © 1972 by Nigel Marsh. Reprinted by permission of Schocken Books Inc.

Sifriyat Rishonom: Elijah David Rabinovitz (Teomim) and Naftali Amsterdam from *Migedole Yerushalayim* by Ya'akov Gellis, Jerusalem, 1967. Copyright © 1967 by Sifriyat Rishonim. Translated for this edition by Nathaniel Stampfer.

Shmuel Tefilinsky from Kuntres Hatzava'a, the ethical will of Rabbi Shmuel Tefilinsky, privately printed by his sons and sons-in-law, Jerusalem, 1968. Translated for this edition by Nathaniel Stampfer.

Dvora Waysman's ethical will originally published by the World Zionist Organization Press Service in 1978. Reprinted by permission of Dvora Waysman.

Yad Vashem Memorial Authority, The Ministry of Education: Among the Embers: Martyrs' Testaments, from *Mime Hashoah Vehagevura,* Jerusalem, 1954/55. Translated for this edition by Nathaniel Stampfer.

Baruch Yashar: Elimelekh of Lisensk and Ben Zion Meir Chai Uziel from *Derech Eretz Venimusim: Sefer Hatzavaot* edited by Baruch Yashar, Jerusalem, 1971. Translated for this edition by Nathaniel Stampfer.

To the memory of my parents
and in honor of my wife's parents,
whose lives are ethical wills—
written not on paper, but in deeds

And to Sue,
partner in all that I am and do.

And to our children—may they have *naches*
from themselves.

—J.R.

To my parents
Elka Stampfer (1893 — 1947)
Samuel Stampfer (1892 — 1981)
who made God's will their own

—N.S.

Contents

PART TWO
Wills from the Holocaust

PART THREE
Wills from the Land of Israel

My father is not dead. My father is a book,
and books do not die.
—Elie Wiesel, *The Testament*

Acknowledgments

Deep gratitude is expressed to the following who have given of their knowledge and skills and otherwise contributed to the publication of this volume: Mr. Joseph Bachrach and the Hebrew Theological College Library, Skokie, Illinois, where he is Assistant Librarian; Charles B. Bernstein, Esq., Chicago, for legal and genealogical counsel; Mrs. Faye Cordell, Skokie; Mr. Dan Sharon and the Norman Asher and Helen Asher Library at Spertus College of Judaica, Chicago, where he is Reference Librarian; my colleague at Spertus College, Dr. Moses A. Shulvass, Distinguished Service Professor of Jewish History; and my beloved and esteemed wife, Dorothy, for insights into difficult aspects of the materials and processes involved in bringing this volume to publication.

We are deeply grateful to the individuals who have shared unpublished wills with us and have allowed us to include them in this volume.

Preface

There is a lovely Jewish custom, one that is unfortunately not sufficiently known in our time—of writing what is called an *ethical will*. Parents would write a letter to their children in which they would try to sum up all that they had learned in life, and in which they would try to express what they wanted most for and from their children. They would leave these letters behind because they believed that the wisdom they had acquired was just as much a part of the legacy they wanted to leave their children as were all the material possessions.

The first ethical wills are found in the Bible. Jacob gathers his children around his bedside and tries to tell them the way in which they should live after he is gone. And Moses makes a farewell address, chastising, prophesying, and instructing his people before he dies. David prepares Solomon before he goes to his eternal rest by warning him whom to be wary of when he becomes king, and by asking him to complete the task he had begun and was unable to complete. The Apocrypha, the Talmud, medieval and modern Hebrew literature all contain examples of ethical wills parents left their children. Many years ago Israel Abrahams published a splendid collection of these medieval wills entitled *Hebrew Ethical Wills*.* We hope this book, which brings together some modern and contemporary wills, will be a fitting continuation of the Abrahams work.

An ethical will is not an easy thing to write. In doing so, one confronts oneself. One must look inward to see what are the essential truths one has learned in a lifetime, face up to one's failures, and consider what are the things that really count. Thus an individual learns a great deal about himself or herself when writing an ethical will. If you had time to write just one letter, to whom would it be addressed? What would it say? What would you leave out? Would you chastise and rebuke? Would you thank, forgive, or seek to instruct?

An ethical will is not an easy thing to read. There is a sense of being a voyeur, of eavesdropping on an intimate conversation, of reading a love letter from the beyond. Although in each case we have been careful to

---

*Israel Abrahams, *Hebrew Ethical Wills* (2 vols.; Philadelphia: Jewish Publication Society, 1926).

obtain permission and have tried to respect privacy, we understand the risk of inquisitiveness that can accompany the reading of these wills. We can only say that those who have chosen to share their innermost thoughts with others have done so out of a sense of responsibility and a desire to teach something out of their experience. Those who read these documents should do so with reverence and with gratitude. We tread carefully here, and we read with a sense of privilege.

An ethical will is not an easy thing to receive. There is the temptation, an almost irresistible one, for parents to try to persuade after death what they were unable to persuade during life. There is the temptation to repeat once more, to plead once more, and to impose a burden of guilt from the grave. The famous and much-quoted letter of Ibn Tibbon is an example of such a castrating and guilt-producing will. Over and over again in his will he berates his child and reminds him how much he has done for him, and then he ends with the instruction that the child should read this will regularly. One can only shudder to think of how much harm such a will can do. One must be able to accept a will as well meant, even if its instructions are sometimes burdensome. One must be able to take it as words that come from the heart and that hopefully enter the heart. One must be able to accept it as an adult receiving instruction from an adult, or else the ties that bind become ties that choke and cripple.

Here, then, are wills of our time. They come from many countries and from many kinds of people. Some were written by scholars, some by simple men and women. Some were written in freedom and safety, from the comfort of a desk, and some were written in trenches and bunkers. Some were written in English, some in Hebrew, Yiddish, or German. All are precious spiritual documents—windows into the souls of those who wrote them.

The four sections of this book reflect the four worlds in which the Jewish people have lived in this century: the world of faith and piety; the world of agony and anguish; the world of return to power and statehood; and the world of freedom. Each of these worlds has presented the Jewish people with a different challenge.

The central spiritual question of the traditional Jews whose wills are contained in the first section of this book was: how to live and how to die *al pi din*—in accordance with the Law. So one rabbi leaves meticulous instructions setting forth precisely what should be done when he dies, by whom, and how, and where. His will contains specific page references to the sources, and precise explanations of where the vestments, the sacred earth, the prayerbooks, and all the rest of the required items will be found. He even leaves precise instructions on how the obituary should be worded, who the attendants should be, what amounts are to be given to which charities in his name, and all the other details that will have to be attended to. With each instruction there is a reference—chapter and verse—to the section on Mourning Procedures in the Law Codes.

For him, and for the other people like him in this section, the tradition was a kind of sacred choreography. *Faith expressed itself in form.* They knew that what has no form has no stability, and no ultimate meaning. The law books by which they governed their lives provided a unified conception of the universe, a conception in which the life and the death of the individual has its place within an eternal order. The people who wrote such wills were leaving more than a catalogue of commandments to their heirs. They were leaving behind a blueprint of existence.

The wills that come out of the Holocaust come out of a very different spiritual atmosphere. They come out of a world in which all the laws had been repealed. It was a world in which faith in God and faith in man went up in smoke together, in which reason and faith both became outdated. What message could a parent send from there to a child outside that would be adequate? What moral could a person send from there that would be appropriate? What word could an inhabitant of that "kingdom of night" send that could be comprehended by one who lived outside?

The wills that come from there resound with the same motifs: "Remember!" "Keep alive what we stood for!" "Don't let us die a second death!" Some are cries for help, based on the naïve belief that those outside did not know, or that if they knew they would care, or that if they cared they could help. Some are letters of resignation from life, expressions of revulsion at living in a world of such brutality. Some are cries for vengeance; who but angels would not want that? And some are cries for continuity, pleas that those outside will pick up the values that they must now put down.

The ethical wills that come from Israel are of a different kind. They are in some cases the farewell letters of young soldiers. They are the words of kibbutzniks or farmers, students or mechanics, young people more at home with a plow or a hammer or a ball than with a pen and paper—or tank and rifle. They are the words of young people who ought to have been dealing with the dilemmas of growing up instead of with the question of how to confront death.

The young Israelis are a taciturn group, not given to excessive senti-mentality. It is for this emotional reserve that they are called "sabras," cactus plants. And yet underneath their tough exteriors there is a hunger for meaning, an awareness of tragedy and absurdity and mortality as constant traveling companions throughout life, and a desire for hope, that come to expression in times of crisis. These letters—which were written on bivouac or scribbled during a break in the battle, or on the eve of a mission—reflect their strivings and yearnings.

A whole new genre of literature has sprung up in Israel. Every kibbutz, every moshav, every high school publishes Memorial Books for the boys whom they have lost in the wars. The books are all similar in style. They contain photographs of the boy growing up, mementoes from his school days, tributes by his friends and family, and then excerpts from his letters, letters in which the tough exterior is bared for a few pages and a questing human being is revealed.

It is significant that while so many of these letters come from what is usually called the "secular" sector of the Israeli community, they contain spritual insights of the highest order. If religion is defined as faith in a God, or in an ordered universe, or as commitment to rituals, or to a regimen of observances, then the boys who wrote these letters were not, strictly speaking, religious people. But if religion is defined another way, not as the possession of truths but as the search for them, or as a way of reaching out beyond oneself, then these letters of the fallen soldiers are religious documents and deserve to be read with reverence.

Two spiritual concerns seem to predominate in the American section. One is the normal natural concern that all people have: that the family stay together, that the name be continued, that the widow be protected, that the values and the bonds of the family be preserved. So, for example, one man, a famous author, asks that his children get together each year on the anniversary of his death and read from his stories, preferably the funny ones. Another man, whose will could not be included here, provided a special trust fund in his estate that would pay the travel costs for his children and grandchildren to come together from wherever they might live, each year, for the family Passover Seder.

And the second motif that appears in many of these wills is: may the Jewish *People* continue. America represents a special challenge to the Jewish people. Never before in our history have we been blessed with as much freedom, as much opportunity, as here. But at the same time, never before in our history have we been challenged by as many alternatives, as many options, as many other ways in which to live. The dilemma facing American Jews is: can we be both part of, and yet apart from, the community around us? Many of these wills are pleas to maintain the balance: to be both participants in American society and good Jews at the same time.

We thank those who have shared these ethical wills with us, and through us, with you.

Jack Riemer

Introduction

The tradition of bequeathing a spiritual legacy either in the form of a codicil to a conventional will or as a separate document has its roots in the Bible and the Talmud. The biblical and talmudic examples, however, are invariably shown to have been conveyed orally while later generations committed their ethical wills to writing. As a result of this practice, numerous examples of *tzavaot* (wills, instructions) of the medieval and Renaissance periods have been preserved. Some of the older ethical wills possess a high literary quality. Others that are not noteworthy in form are exquisite in their content.

But literary integrity was not primary in the intentions of the writers of ethical wills. Deeply cherished was the desire to bequeath to their descendants an instructive account of the ideals and *midot* (traits, measures of refinement) closest to their hearts. They sought to write and transmit not philosophical treatises but personal reflections on their lives as Jews and on the motivating values and events in their life's experience. They hoped to impart the precepts of God's Law refracted through the prism of a parent's life. While the writing of ethical wills is not unknown to the Christian and Muslim traditions, this volume is devoted exclusively to Jewish ethical wills.

As with material possessions, parents often conveyed the ethical inheritance *during* their lifetimes. In this context, an ethical testament may be referred to as an *iggeret* (letter, missive); the term is thus used in the present volume. Many ethical wills are thought to have been conveyed during the lifetimes of their authors. Clearly these are ultimately identical to those conveyed posthumously and may be so regarded for all purposes; they too speak from "beyond the grave" and become *tzavaot* upon the death of the writer. The intentions are certainly identical and for these reasons no distinction is made between *igrot* (plural of *iggeret*) and *tzavaot* in this collection.

As noted in the Preface to this volume, the first collection of ethical wills, *Hebrew Ethical Wills,* was published in America by the British scholar Israel Abrahams.* The present collection differs from the pioneer

---

*Israel Abrahams, *Hebrew Ethical Wills* (2 vols.; Philadelphia: Jewish Publication Society, 1926).

work of Professor Abrahams in several respects. A major distinction lies in the intent of the authors of this anthology: to compile a representative sample of the ethical wills literature of the modern period. Thus this collection contains wills by rabbis and prominent leaders as well as those of unknown or relatively obscure individuals. Further, the wills in this collection are drawn entirely from the modern period (i.e., post – French Revolution)—the earliest is dated 1787; the Abrahams work closes with the will of R. Joel ben Avraham Shemaria, published in 1799 or 1800.

The ethical wills presented here fall under four headings: traditional testaments, wills from the Holocaust, from Israel, and by contemporary American Jews. The reader will quickly discover that the difference in historical time frames and the events they brought produces significant additions and changes in the concerns expressed by the writers of ethical wills, and in the languages used as well. Wills of the modern period are written in the vernacular more often than in Hebrew, notably Yiddish, German, and English. Last but no means least, women in the modern period have begun to make contributions that deserve to be treasured as part of Jewish ethical wills literature.

Several points need to be made about the rabbinical ethical wills in this collection. Whether in the form of *hanhagot*—rules for daily ritual and ethical conduct—or as essays on ethical behavior woven about a mosaic of biblical and talmudic passages, rabbinical wills are not written for the families of the writers alone. The rabbis' commitments extend beyond their immediate family circles, and most often are not limited even to the extended family of the congregation. Rabbis and *bnei Torah,* scholars whose lives are devoted to the sacred lore and its observance, often speak to all the Congregation of the Children of Israel in all generations. Hence their testaments include, in addition to messages directed to their own kindred, ethical insights addressed to Jews everywhere. As rabbinical wills tend to be lengthy (the complete will of Reb Shmuel Tefilinsky contains forty-five pages), meaningful selections from their contents often tend to be lengthy. The authors have not hesitated to present these longer selections where necessary to preserve the structure of *tzavaot* that are classic examples of the genre.

Finally, we are not free to desist from addressing some thoughts to the research-oriented reader. The studious reader will come away from a careful reading of ethical wills, especially a collection as representative as this one, with a number of seminal questions: What are the persistent themes that pervade this literature? Are these sustained over the generations, everywhere, or are they confined to divisions of time and space? How is the influence of surrounding cultures reflected? In language and style? In changing patterns of emphasis regarding certain personal-ethical traits? What is the relationship between ethical wills literature and other contemporaneous ethics literature? Such questions may well lead to the formulation of hypotheses that can support significant analytic studies.

Further, as a popular ("originating among the people") literary genre, ethical wills, perhaps more than most writings, record many little-known Jewish rituals, optional in nature, hallowed by certain families and within some ideological enclaves. Among these are: fashioning one's bier out of boards from one's Sabbath table, and distributing alms in amounts equaling the numerical value of the letters in one's Hebrew name. Another compilation, of interest to language specialists but to others as well, is that of biblical and talmudic paraphrases. Such paraphrases are well rooted in all Jewish languages and vernaculars, but the origins are largely unknown by the users. Conversely, phrases abound that are erroneously attributed to classical Jewish sources.

These latter examples suggest the descriptive types of study that may be undertaken with profit. The ethical wills literature is of sufficient size to justify and sustain such studies as those touched on above. Our selection is not exhaustive but is representative of published *tzavaot* of the modern period and of the contemporary wills which families have kindly permitted us to share with the public.

Nathaniel Stampfer

Part One

TRADITIONAL WILLS

*The designation of the wills in the following section as "traditional" does not imply uniformity in form or content, as even a cursory reading reveals. The unifying element is their focus on the traditional precepts and values of Judaism, including Torah study, observance of rituals and the socioethical precepts, and striving for perfection by developing the virtues exemplified in the lives of biblical and historic Jewish personalities and through imitation of the Divine Attributes. The exhortations toward these values, however, take various forms—letters to loved ones (*igrot*), rules for the daily conduct of the pious (*hanhagot*), elaborate suggestions for ideal methods of study, and others. A unifying geographic thread appears to prevail in that most of the wills in this section were written by Jews in Europe.*

So bald mein Hinscheiden eingetreten ist, so mögen meine Schüler es mir zu Liebe thun um — טהרה — ... משעת פטירתי ... לזכות נשמתי

Ich verlange jedoch nicht, daß dieses במקום פטירתי geschehe, um Niemand belästigen mag, sondern sie können es auch in ihrer Wohnung thun. Von der טהרה ... bis zur Kindheit מצהרב mögen 2 meiner Schüler lernen, (die also dann nicht mit hinaus gehen sollen), במקום פטירתי .

מנין soll nur stattfinden während der שבעה und auch gelernt werden aus meinen משניות ; ich möchte aber nicht, daß dies von bezahlten Leuten geschehe. —

Dann richte ich die Bitte an meine zahlreichen Schüler, daß alle die im Stande sind und den Willen haben, לזכות את נשמתי , während der ganzen יב חדש Morgens und abends abends mindestens eine משנה mit dem פירוש הרע״ב lernen. Die dies nicht können, mögen jeden Morgen und jeden Abend mindestens ein Capitel תהלים sagen. Alle, die dies thun, mögen vorher sagen:

הנני לומד זאת לזכות נשמת שמשון בן אורי שרגא

Für תהלים :

הנני אומר זאת לזכות נשמת שמשון בן אורי שרגא

תנוח דעתכם שהנחתם את דעתי

Als Dank sage ich denselben im Voraus.

Dann ersuche ich die Vereine מקור חיים und אוהל יצחק , denen ich so viele Jahre angehört habe, stets meiner Jahrzeit und der meiner Frau זכרונה לברכה zu gedenken, indem sie einen besonderen שיעור משניות lernen und nachsagen קדיש דרבנן . Ich hoffe auch die Gewährung dieser Bitte. —

The ethical will of Dr. Samson Nathan.

Samson M. Nathan

Dr. Samson Nathan (1820 – 1906) was an instructor of Bible and Talmud as well as mathematics and physics at the Talmud Torah-Realschule in Hamburg. Although he received ordination from the leading rabbis in Germany and earned a doctorate at the University of Jena, he rejected all offers to occupy rabbinic positions. His greatest desire was to be a teacher and he taught uninterruptedly for fifty-seven years in his native city. Besides teaching at the Realschule, he served as judge on the rabbinic court of Hamburg and for many years taught the two adult study fellowships mentioned in his will.

Hamburg, Germany

As soon as I have passed away my students may do me the kindness, for the uplift of my soul, to study [Torah] from the moment of my death until the purification rite. But I do not request that they do this at the place where I expire because I do not wish to impose a burden on anyone. So they may do this in their own homes. From the time of the purification until returning from the cemetery, two of my students may remain to study; therefore they need not go along. The minyan-quorum for prayer should be conducted at the place of my death, but only during the week of *shivah* [mourning] and the studying should be done from my own Mishnah volumes. I would not like this study to be done through paid individuals.

Further, I beg of my many students that whoever is able and has the desire to uplift my soul should study at least one Mishnah with the *Bertoniro* commentary during the twelve months, morning and evening. Those unable to do so may recite at least one Psalm morning and evening. Anyone doing so may first recite: "I hereby do this for the purification of the soul of Shim'on ben Uri Shraga." As thanks I say to them in advance: "Be assured that you have reassured me" [*Shabbat* 152b; *Yoma* 66b].

I also beg of the associations Ohel Yitzhak and Mekor Hayyim, with which I was associated many years, to observe my *yahrzeit* [anniversary of death] and that of my wife of blessed memory by conducting a special Mishnah session and to recite the Rabbinic Kaddish afterward. I hope this wish will be complied with.

Elimelekh of Lisensk

Reb Elimelekh of Lisenk (1717 – 1787) was a disciple of the Maggid of Mezeritch. He was the founder of the Hasidic movement in Galicia and author of Noam Elimelekh, *published posthumously, in which the doctrine of the Zaddik (the hasidic rabbi as saint and wonder worker) finds its fullest expression. The following are selections from "A Little Note," which he left at his death, written in the form of* hanhagot, *rules of ethical conduct. Prayerbooks often contain selections from this source.*

One must accustom himself never to initiate conversation with anyone for other than what is urgently required. Even then one should speak but few words, carefully sifted and screened so that there be no trace of untruth in his speech, God forbid, nor offense, gossip, slander, insult, nor any manner of ostentation. And one should train himself according to the rule of the sages, "Teach your tongue to say 'I do not know'" [Tractate *Berakhot* 4b; *Derekh Eretz Zuta,* Chapter 3].

When engaged in conversation with individuals who are not careful about idle talk, let him evade them with all his might and by any stratagem; and when it is impossible to extricate himself by any means, let him at least keep to a minimum what it is that he must answer them.

One must guard against disliking any fellow Jew except the wicked who are definitely known to him to be beyond judgment in the scale of merit. But if it *is* possible to judge them in the scale of merit [i.e., by reason of benefit of the doubt] then one is duty-bound to love them with all his might, as himself, fulfilling the admonition ". . . love thy neighbor as thyself. . . ."

Above all: Let one guard against intoxicating drink, for this is a vile disease that can lead to extreme degradation. In the words of the talmudic sage, ". . . do not imbibe and you will not sin."

Also, one should guard against conversing at all in the synagogue, even words of moral instruction, lest he be led thereby to indulge in idle speech.

David ben Meir Friesenhausen

*The Enlightenment (*haskalah, *in Hebrew) which swept Europe from West to East following the French Revolution affected the Jew profoundly. Its impact on traditional Jews was varied—some retreated before the waves of modernity into a more sequestered Judaism; others abandoned the traditions of their fathers. Still others developed a distinctive synthesis of the old and new cultures mediated by Hebrew and Yiddish translations of scientific and humanistic classical works, and by university studies heretofore denied them. These selections, from the ethical will of a scholarly Bavarian Jew, a* maskil, *represent a remarkable synthesis between faithful adherence to religious tradition and studious pursuit of mathematics and the sciences.*

The will of David ben Meir Friesenhausen (c. 1750 – 1828) is found in his book Mosedot Tevel *(Foundations of the Universe), published in 1820. Part I of his book explains the Copernican rules of planetary motion and Part II is a detailed treatise on Euclidean geometry. Both are presented for the first time in Hebrew, according to the author. The third and final part of the book is his ethical will, whose content reflects the synthesis of traditional and scientific insights achieved by the author.*

These are things you shall do, then will God be beneficent to you and to your children after you.

1. When a child is born to you, be very careful the first thirty days when the infant sleeps in his mother's bed, to prevent the sleeping mother from rolling over on the child and suffocating it. Similarly, prevent the infant from sleeping face-down or having a pillow fall on its face. Also, alert the nurse to keep watch over the child at night. After thirty days the child can be put to sleep in its own crib.

2. Hurry, without delay, to save your children from the deadly smallpox by giving them the illness called *cowpox,* which saves human beings from the more dangerous smallpox. As is now well known, this is a proven treatment, demonstrated by tens and hundreds of thousands of children; there is no doubt about it whatsoever, thank God, and no danger is connected with it.

I know that some of our leaders regarded as wise and pious have forbidden cowpox infusion, but this is due to error. Their mistake stems from the fact that earlier treatments used to utilize matter from children who were only mildly ill of smallpox to treat unaffected children as a preventive. Some of the children so treated sometimes died from this treatment, so the rabbis banned it, rightly. But the more modern treatment, with cowpox, is different. All that happens is that a slight fever develops, and then the child is immune to smallpox. No one is known to have died from this treatment. Of course, if the child already has the disease in his body before the treatment, it cannot *cure* him. For this reason, parents must treat children as early as possible. And let us thank God, Who performs wonders, for enlightening our eyes to this cure, saving multitudes from untimely death.

3. Our sages have stated that the period for nursing children is two years, but physicians in our day say there is no need for this—it is too troublesome for the mother—and many people listen to them. Now, you, my offspring, if you love your children, do not listen to these physicians, and do not deviate from the teachings of our sages. Because during the first two years the child is subject to various diseases. Experience teaches that during illness and fever the child will not reject the mother's milk which will then sustain his life. Therefore listen to me, my daughters and daughters-in-law: do not wean your children before two years unless you know yourself to be with child or if you are too weak physically to nurse.

4. When the child begins to speak it will be in the language of his parents or others in his environment. Since Hebrew is essential for the Jew, both for sons and daughters alike to understand the daily prayers and supplications, it is important to teach them Hebrew verbs and nouns and to explain the meanings of all the prayers as soon as they are able to grasp them.

When boys are ready for learning, this is the sequence of study:

1. The Five Books of Moses, translated and explained, without commentaries;
2. Early Prophets and the Scrolls of Ruth and Esther;
3. Daniel, Ezra, Nehemiah, and Chronicles;
4. Later Prophets and the Scroll of Lamentations;
5. The Writings, and the Scrolls of Ecclesiastes and Song of Songs.

In conjunction with these text studies it is beneficial to teach Hebrew grammar, for it is unseemly for Torah scholars, great and small, to be ignorant on this subject. I have seen great scholars ignorant about grammar who were therefore unable to cope with certain passages; those not knowing these rules find various explanations of Rashi and other commentaries closed before them.

And because students find it easier to grasp a language in youth than in later years, as experience shows, do not neglect to teach your sons and daughters the language of the land. So long as the Jew does not dwell in his own land, and God has not gathered His dispersed people, it is very important to learn the language of the nation in whose midst we dwell.

5. At seven years, examine the child to determine whether he is endowed with the intellect to learn and understand the Talmud. If he is, initiate the studies, but slowly, moving from the easier to the more difficult. And because the purpose of studying the Law is the observance of the precepts therein, the emphasis of studies from ages seven to thirteen should be on Tractate [Talmud volume] *Berakhot* and the Order of Festivals, for in these are encompassed the regular rituals of Jewish life enumerated in the Orah Hayyim section of the Code of Jewish Law. These should be known accurately and in detail by every Jew. Do not confuse the lad with excessive commentary—it is sufficient for him to study each topic with Rashi, Tosafot, and the Maharsha commentaries, according to his capacity.

From thirteen to seventeen or eighteen let him learn the tractates and topics relating to the Yoreh De'ah section [dealing with dietary laws, etc.] of the Code of Jewish Law.

From the age of eighteen onward he can begin to learn the Order of Torts and the Order of Women, along with the two remaining sections of the Code associated with them.

Inasmuch as I have already informed you earlier that knowledge of the sciences is necessary for one's spiritual integrity, and since the sciences are well elucidated only in these three languages—German, French, and English—the cultivated person should learn at least one of these three. So let each one choose the one that for him is easier than the others.

Along with language study it is well to include study of the five fields of mathematics. Also the written form of all languages studied should be mastered. It is important that the student be skilled in writing for it is essential for all human enterprise, be it for sacred lore, the sciences, or commercial endeavor.

With the study of Talmud, it is fitting for every God-fearing person in his youth to spend one hour each day in the study of *musar* [moral] literature. This will help acquaint him with the principles which lead to ethical excellence in the sight of God and in relating to all men.

It is well for the teacher to instruct even the very young in moral paths so that these can be deeply engraved on their hearts. The most precious of these books of *musar* is *Hovot Halevavot* [*Duties of the Heart*] of Rabbi Bahya ibn Pakuda, of blessed memory. But there are books in other languages as well, called "morality books," about one's responsibility toward God and toward fellowman. It is good to read from these books too, from time to time, because they present their ideas attractively through fables and events from very ancient days. They make no mention of religion at all, but speak only of man's achieving happiness by being virtuous in God's sight and dealing honestly with people. When they do mention religion it is only to point out that each person should observe the ways of his own faith, and not to be a savage. However, books that teach about one particular religion are called "theologie," and with these we have no reason to become involved.

6. If you determine for certain that the lad is not suited to Talmud study, lacking in grasp, perception, and memory, then his major study will be confined to Scripture, *musar,* and Codes, knowledge he will need for his guidance all his life. When he reaches the age of thirteen, teach him a trade so that he may earn his livelihood by the work of his hands. While one cannot achieve wealth through labor, still he can earn enough for all his needs. And if he is sufficiently skillful at his craft, he may combine it with some trade or business under the statutes of the land of his sojourn. In this way he can earn his living honorably, and serve his God in truth and honor. Therefore I say it is well for the lad to learn writing and arithmetic, for there is no enterprise in the world that does not require these skills.

7. If the lad *is* successful in his Talmud studies, he must still be taught a good vocation, unless he chooses to make the study of the Sacred Lore

his lifelong pursuit. Others among the great scholars have done so with great success, others not so successfully. Perhaps the latter were not completely dedicated to such study for its own sake. On the other hand many of our greatest sages in the Talmud combined their studies with a trade. This seems good; for how can a nation exist without professional artisans to ply the crafts needed by society? Also, when the Almighty gathers the dispersed of Israel, we too will require all kinds of skilled craftsmen; and if we are then as we are now, I do not know how our country will function. Will God make windows in the heavens and lower some craftsmen to earth? Or shall we import them from the surrounding nations? This is not a good situation. I myself have often bemoaned the fact that I did not learn a trade in my youth.

8. On the subject of training and educating the girls, it is somewhat simpler since they are exempt from Torah study. But they must be taught to read Hebrew as well as the language of the surrounding people, to understand the meanings of the prayers which they must pray, the writing of the national language, and the skills of arithmetic. Then the skills of baking, cooking, washing, and weaving, and all necessary domestic skills. With all this do not neglect to instruct them in the moral and ethical paths relating one to God and to man. One must teach his daughter how to act as a wife, to be faithful, to listen, and not to be contrary about everything so long as her husband acts according to the Jewish faith, not to revile him but to speak gently and in an advice-giving tone. But beware, my children, of giving your daughter in marriage to someone whom she does not desire; and do not let monetary considerations be a factor in these matters, but only good qualities of physical and spiritual integrity, which are the only true definitions of a human being.

9. Since our exile from our own land we have not fought in the wars of people in whose midst we dwelt. But now, in recent years, the yoke of exile has been lightened, thank God, and we are no longer like sheep led to slaughter; [there is] one uniform statute and law for all subjects of the king. We are equal to all others. With this, government laws now also apply to Jews with regard to military service, as to all others. As you know, my children, I believe that all that happens under the sun happens by Providence; and this too, I am certain in my heart, is ultimately for the good of our people. I have no way of knowing whether any of my

offspring will be involved in this network of events. But I admonish each of you beforehand that if so, you are to avoid violating any of God's commandments except under life-or-death circumstances. This also do, and live: learn well the rules and tactics of making war; but remember, we are *Kohanim,* priests to the Lord our God, whom God elevated to sacred service to be leaders of our people and to be their guides.

10. As I have stated, it is proper to have an honest vocation. Now the science of medicine is one of the many professions that sustains its practitioners and earns wealth and respect for one who excels in it, besides carrying with it the reward of long life. Therefore, any male descended of me who is not a *Kohen,* or anyone not a *Kohen* marrying a daughter or granddaughter of mine, who feels endowed with the needed intelligence and insight, let him pursue this profession. But let him labor very hard to master its every intricacy and innermost content.

Why do I condition my advice on not being a *Kohen?* Because I am aware that one cannot plumb the depths of medical practice without mastering the science of anatomy, of internal and external limbs and organs. As a *Kohen* one is prohibited from contact with a cadaver, without which mastery of anatomy seems unattainable. If, however, one can master this science without touching corpses, then even a *Kohen* should be able to pursue the study of medicine.

11. In summary: In light of all the things in this will which I bequeath you and your descendants, you will perceive that my sole purpose and heart's desire are to help you achieve happiness throughout your years of life in this world and to earn for you eternal life and a good end in the next.

Regarding the latter, you cannot attain it unless you walk in God's paths and observe His commandments, His statutes, and His laws as taught us by Moses, our teacher.

As to the former, you can achieve it by avoiding the habit of sloth, and develop diligence in all your undertakings; execute all your enterprises in good faith whether in your own vicinity or far from home.

Finally, because any man who truly loves mankind is not content merely with his own happiness and that of his own offspring, he should strongly desire and seek the happiness of all others.

Solomon Kluger

Rabbi Solomon Kluger (1785 – 1869), one of the most gifted talmudists and halakhists of the modern era, was the rabbi of Brody for nearly fifty years. Brody (also Brod) was a substantial city and a Jewish center on the border between Russia and Austrian Galicia. During the 1880s it was the transfer point for Jews seeking to settle in the West, much like Vienna a century later for Soviet Jews emigrating westward. Rabbi Kluger's career coincided with decades of intense activity of the Haskalah (Enlightenment) Movement. His strong support of tradition against changes sought by proponents of haskalah is reflected in the sections of his will translated here. As a youth, following the death of his father, rabbi of Komarov, he studied in Zamosc under Rabbi Jacob Kranz, the renowned Maggid of Dubno. Rabbi Kluger, known also by the mnemonic Maharshak, was a remarkably prolific author—his known writings include 175 works in addition to hundreds of responsa. The younger son, Abraham Benjamin, mentioned in the first addendum to the following will, succeeded his father as rabbi of Brody. The provision for the ritual of stoning described in the final codicil is uncommon but not unique in the ethical wills literature.

Because this year I enter my Jubilee [fiftieth] Year, I have thought perhaps the Almighty will cleanse me of my transgressions through his love and mercy and not through suffering; by His mercies let him purify me as I was at birth, and thus restore my soul to its pristine inheritance, as Scripture states, "In this year of jubilee ye shall return every man unto his possession" (Lev. 25:13). Who knows whether I shall be clear-minded when my time comes and responsible for my actions. I have decided, therefore, to plan my journey now. "The preparations of the heart are man's, but the answer of the tongue is from the Lord" (Prov. 16:1).

Let me begin by discussing how to prepare "provisions for the journey,"* may the Almighty in His kindness guide me toward good.

When those who stand near me sense that the departure of my soul is imminent, let them assemble ten pious men, and let them prevent anyone, including my wife and children, from approaching my bed closer than four cubits.

*In hasidic lore the expression "provisions for the journey" refers to the good deeds accumulated during a man's lifetime, since these sustain him during life after death.

Afterward, remove my body directly onto the earth, if I am near bare earth at the time. But if there is a wooden or stone floor, let them bring earth from somewhere (preferably from the synagogue courtyard or from the house of study, or another clean, pure place nearby) and sprinkle it on the floor. Then place my body directly on the earth with nothing intervening.

Take two books of mine that I wrote with the skills with which God endowed me, whichever two chance first to come to hand. Open them, place them face down, one over my heart and one on my head, covering my eyes and forehead. Then cover over everything the same as is customarily done for everyone.

For the time of *teharah* [ritual cleansing of the body] I shall consider it a true kindness if those who perform it go first to the *mikvah* [ritual pool]. After the *teharah,* let them try to obtain some earth from Eretz Yisrael [the Land of Israel]. Perhaps God will enable me to prepare some for myself by then. If not, let them seek some. First let them place some on the sign of the sacred covenant; if any remains, let them sprinkle some on my heart; if some remains, place some on my eyes; then if any is left, sprinkle it on my forehead, on the place of the tefillin [phylacteries]. If, God forbid, they cannot find any earth from Eretz Yisrael, let them take earth from the floor of the synagogue and put it on the above places, and let them recite: "May it be Thy will, O Lord our God, that this may serve in place of earth from the Holy Land to atone for this person, Shlomo Ya'akov Yosef ben Yehuda." It would be good if this earth is from the place in the synagogue where the reader stands.

Before removing me outdoors, announce a prohibition forbidding my wife and child from accompanying me to my grave and against their approaching closer than four cubits to my grave during the first twelve months. Afterward, this prohibition is nullified. I hereby instruct my wife and son to observe the above in keeping with the rules of reverence for parents and under the most stringent injunction.

When they have taken me outside, anounce that I gave instructions before my death to ask forgiveness from all against whom I may have erred, in word or deed, whether in the course of rendering judgments or in business affairs; and if I aggravated anyone in any way, I ask them to forgive and pardon me. Then let each one say quietly that he forgives me for everything. And I do the same regarding them.

As for a eulogy, I do not restrain anyone from the *mitzvah* [divine commandment, or any worthy deed] of eulogizing who may be moved to do so. But only on condition that no specific praise be said referring expressly to me. Only in a general way, mentioning some sayings of the sages and mentioning the great merit of speaking about and weeping over the death of a worthy human being. But avoid mentioning me directly in connection with words of praise or worthiness. Just say, "This man served the public for many years, and now it is fitting that we perform these services for him," and "We beseech the Almighty in his behalf to forgive his transgressions and set him on the path of goodness and life."

Now you, my comrade, my son, of you I request that you recite the Kaddish for me with great devotion and deliberation. Make every effort to serve as reader morning and evening in the synagogue, pray with devotion, and be sure to study a regular lesson in Mishnah or Gemara, then to recite the "Yehi Ratzon" for the uplift of my soul, as it is printed in the prayerbooks; then recite the Rabbis' Kaddish with deliberation and heartfelt devotion.

Be very careful to honor your mother, and certainly never to irritate her, as the Torah requires of you. And likewise teach your wife to honor your mother.

Seek also to honor me after my death in every way possible, and for Heaven's sake, tread the paths of righteousness, be God-fearing, depart from evil, and do good [Pss. 34:15, 37:27].

Do not be among those erring moderns, neither of this extreme group or another; just walk in the path of moderation, the way of our fathers.

But in one thing put forth great effort—do not depart from the Code of Religious Law—right or left; then will you prosper and succeed, and merit seeing your children and your children's children engaged in Torah pursuits.

Let your heart be perfect with the Almighty; do not engage in philosophical probings, but recite daily the Thirteen Principles with utmost devotion, and thereby will you be strengthened and not falter; you will know that the ways of God are beyond us, and that all is created by Him, blessed be He, so it is not for man to investigate His deeds. So do not be envious of this group or the other that pursue such a course with apparent success, for so it is foreordained, that before the coming of the Redeemer, falsehood is allowed to triumph just prior to its final extinction, the same as a candle flame flares brightest just before it goes out. All this is a true test for those who stand firm in their faith in God and in the principles of His Torah.

Do not turn aside right or left for the sake of illusory success. Give heed to all these matters about which I instruct you briefly here, because it is impossible to elaborate it fully in writing.

May the Lord be your help to guide you in paths straight and good in His eyes; and may you live to one hundred twenty years and live to see the Redeemer soon and in our day. Amen.

On my tombstone let no virtues be inscribed, nor any titles, only:

Here lies our teacher, Rabbi Shlomo, judge in the community of Brody, son of the Light of the Exile, our saintly teacher Rabbi Judah, his memory for eternal life, judge in Komarov.

Do not inscribe "righteous judge" because God alone knows whether I judged aright; therefore merely inscribe "judge." Avoid writing about virtues,* because what is the good of a Song of Ascents? It is the purpose of man to be an acceptable offering on God's altar. It is written too, "Neither shalt thou ascend by steps unto my altar . . ." (Ex. 20:23), for it is not because of praises said of him in this world that a man ascends to the altar of God, blessed be He. On the contrary, ". . . that thy nakedness be not uncovered thereon" (Ex. 20:23); excessive extolling here may cause more [scrutiny of] shortcomings on high. Therefore avoid mentioning

---

*These passages constitute a brief, clever homily based on a play on words, namely, the three meanings of the word *ma'alot:* virtues, ascents, and steps. Paraphrased, the homily reads, "Do not speak of my virtues [*ma'alot*], for what good is a 'Song of Ascents' [*Shir Hama'alot*, Psalms 120– 134]; one does not ascend the altar by these steps [*ma'alot*]."

in a eulogy or inscribing on a tombstone any praise of virtues; and I pray that my shortcomings may be overlooked and my transgressions covered over by His love.

These are the words of the writer, whose sighs pour forth from a breaking heart, Thursday, I Adar 4, 5594 [February 14, 1834], in Brody.

This ends the text of the original will of Rabbi Kluger. Codicils were added to the original in 1848 and 1852 of which the following are excerpts. A third codicil, added in 1854, deals with material bequests and is not represented here.

Added in 5608 (1848)

I have already written a will, with God's help, in 1834. But conditions have changed, since my first wife has died and I have since remarried. Also, I have a child with her, thank God; may He enable him to attain to Torah study, to marriage, and to good deeds. For these reasons I must alter some of the material provisions enumerated there.

My books as well as my unpublished manuscripts shall be divided equally between my two sons. I beg my [elder] son Hayyim Yehuda, and enjoin him with the admonition of paternal reverence never to vex my wife nor my son, the lad Master Avraham Binyamin, and to fulfill the dictum of the sages, "'Honor thy father and thy mother' is to include the father's wife as well." Be as a father to the lad and watch over him in every way necessary, for as you know, the lad was my delight, "brought up in scarlet" [Lam. 4:5], and I cannot endure the thought of his suffering pain or distress, God forbid. And I promise my [elder] son that should I succeed in being a spokesman for him on high, I shall certainly be an advocate in his behalf.

So too do I ask of all my loved ones and my friends to be alert in every way possible in watching over the child and guiding him along the proper path and toward worthy objectives. For this may the Almighty reward them, as this is an act of true kindness.*

Let all other matters be carried out as explained in my original will.

---

*The expression "acts of true kindness," *hesed shel emet,* is reserved in Jewish tradition for kindnesses done for the deceased, since they are done without expectation of any reward.

Added 5613 (1852)

Sunday, Heshvan 18, 5613 [Oct. 31, 1852]

I further request that my grave be next to anyone at all, so long as it is someone known to be a thoroughly upright man and poor; and do not bury me next to a wealthy person even if he is known to be completely upright. Also, do not bury a wealthy person next to me [later] even if he is known to be upright, but only a poor man known to be upright; and attired as Jews are supposed to be;* and also, he should not be an enemy to me nor I to him.

I also prohibit my wife and children from approaching my grave closer than four cubits. But my grandchildren, both male and female, and my daughters-in-law are permitted to approach my grave.

Be aware that there is [prepared] a piece of rock, and it is of earth from Eretz Yisrael. See that it is crushed and placed on the organs listed in my will. But purchase some soil from Eretz Yisrael as well, because who knows which is truly from there. So put them both on, and if you mix them both together it would be better still.

I instruct my sons to recite the Kaddish in the twelfth month as well; and if it should be a leap year, then the thirteenth month as well, up until the date of the anniversary.†

When they remove my body [from the deathbed] to place me on the earth, let them throw me down from the bed onto the ground. Then let them take a large stone and throw it on my heart, not gently but forcefully, as they recite, "Lord, full of compassion, have mercy upon this deceased; let this be accounted unto him as though he were subject to stoning by the Sanhedrin, by virtue of his intention while writing [his will] in conjunction with this present act. Let this be accounted unto him as though the Sanhedrin sentenced him to all four capital punishments

*I.e., in white shroud and prayer shawl.

†Kaddish is customarily recited the first eleven months after the death. The reason for this is that according to mystic lore, the dead who are sinful require twelve months to become purified in Gehinnom; the Kaddish, which helps alleviate the sufferings of the deceased during that process, is therefore recited only *eleven* months for loved ones in order not to categorize them as sinful. The author here states clearly that he wishes to have the Kaddish recited for the full year since no man knows what grievous sins he may have unwittingly committed. Also, leap years in the Hebrew calendar contain an extra month, and the writer provides for such an eventuality as well.

[stoning, burning, slaying, strangling] for we have it on the authority of the rabbis that the punishment of stoning is the most severe. Thus may this man be purified of all his defects.* In the Name of the Four Letters of the Tetragrammaton, may it be His will."

*In ancient Jewish law, capital punishment could be imposed for specified offenses by one of four modes of execution: stoning, burning, slaying (by the sword), and strangulation. So many strictures surrounded its application, however, that capital punishment was seldom employed, and was abolished entirely forty years before the destruction of the Second Temple (Babylonian Talmud, *Makkot* 7a). Nevertheless Rabbi Kluger requests the symbolic stoning after death in case he had been inadvertently culpable during his lifetime. His choice of stoning over the other modes on grounds that it was the most severe refers to the gravity of the offenses that call for stoning, for stoning was reserved for such transgressions as blasphemy, rebelliousness, and idolatry, all of which deny the existence of God, a sine qua non of Judaism (Babylonian Talmud *Sanhedrin* 49b).

Moses Sofer (Hatam Sofer)

Rabbi Moses Sofer (1762 – 1839) was the rabbi of Pressburg for thirty-three years, when it was the foremost Jewish community in Hungary. The yeshiva which he headed was the largest since the days of the Babylonian academies. He was universally recognized for profound scholarship, high moral character, and superb qualities of leadership. Throughout his career he opposed the antitraditional influences emanating from the West—the Enlightenment and liberal trends within Judaism. The cryptic reference to Moses Mendelssohn in the selections from his will presented here underscores his attitudes toward the "innovators." His attitude toward tradition is evident from the fact that he regarded all Jewish customs hallowed by time and usage to have equal binding force with biblical commandments. He was one of the Orthodox leaders who believed in and encouraged the settlement of Eretz Yisrael.

Kislev 15, 5597 [1837]

As no man knows his allotted time, it is always time to perform divine service, that is, Torah study, exalting God's House, restoring the ruins; you, my sons and daughters, my sons-in-law, grandchildren, and their children, hearken and flourish.

Incline not to enter into disputations with or make charges against those wrongdoers who have arisen of late who have separated themselves from God and His Torah. Do not dwell in their vicinity and do not associate with them at all. Have nothing to do with the books of R.M.D.* ever, then your foot will not slip.

Study the Scriptures with the Rashi commentary, and Pentateuch with the Ramban [Nachmanides] commentary; you yourselves will benefit, and teach it to your children, for he [Nachmanides] is foremost in faithfulness and truth,† and through him you will become wiser than Calcol, Darda, and Heman.‡ Even, heaven forbid, at the cost of hunger, thirst and poverty, stand firm and do not turn to these idols [Lev. 19:4] and do not eliminate God from your consciousness.

*Meaning Rabbi Moses Dessauer (Moses Mendelssohn), against whose influences Rabbi Sofer struggled throughout his career.
†Paraphrase of Isaiah 25:1.
‡Allusion to I Kings 5:11, "For he [Solomon] was wiser than all men . . . than Heman, and Calcol, and Darda, the sons of Mahol."

Let your daughters study from the German [Yiddish] books written in our [Hebrew] characters [*hagofen shelanu*, Tractate *Megillah* 9a], that are based on the agadic writings of the sages, and nothing beyond that.

Never set foot into theaters, heaven forbid. I enjoin you on this by absolute prohibition; and may you be privileged to behold the graciousness of the Lord [Ps. 27:4] when He causes His children to rejoice, soon and in our day, Amen.

If the Almighty raises you up to success and sees fit to favor you, as I hope He will, do not lift your heads in pride or arrogance, God forbid, toward any upright person. Know that we are the children of Abraham our father, disciples of Moses our teacher, and the subjects of David our king. Our father said, ". . . I am but dust and ashes" [Gen. 18:27]. Our teacher said, ". . . and what are we?" [Ex. 16:7]. Our king said, ". . . I am but a worm and not a man" [Ps. 22:7]. Furthermore, the hoped-for king [the Messiah] will reveal himself in the guise of a poor man riding on a donkey! In view of all this, whence conceit and pride?

Be strong and courageous in diligent and penetrating study of God's law. Establish groups for the dissemination of Torah, and promote activities for Torah among the populace. If you can do only a little, then do that little with utmost devotion, in a way that you will know in your heart that the Almighty knows there are no mixed motives on your part, [that you do it] for the sake of His great name alone. For ". . . a hypocrite cannot come before Him" [Job 13:16].

Beware of altering your Jewish names, language, and attire. A clue to this is found in the verse, "Jacob arrived in peace (*shalem*) at Shechem" [Gen. 33:18].*

Do not be concerned if you are not endowed with a fortune, because the Father of Orphans will have compassion and mercy for those bereft of father and mother, and He will not forsake you. There is no limit in God's ability to help, much or little, as needed.

Do not make of God's Torah a spade with which to dig,† heaven

---

*A mnemonic based on the word *shalem*, whose three radical letters, *Sh, L,* and *M* represent *SHem* = name, *Lashon* = language, *Malbush* = attire. The author lists three external manifestations of Jewish identity which he instructs his followers to preserve. This injunction reflects similar lists found in the midrashic literature enumerating traits and conduct which helped the Israelites preserve their identity in Egypt.

†Paraphrase of *Avot* 4:7.

forbid, much less go about preaching for pay, or begging to be hired. For it [your due] is being held in your name, and in your rightful place will you be installed, and that which is intended for you will you receive [Tractate *Yoma* 35a].

Do not say, "The times have changed," for we have our Father of yore, blessed be His name, Who has not changed and Who will not change. No evil shall befall you, and you will be blessed from Him Who is our eternal dwelling place.

Moshe Hakatan Sofer of Frankfort-am-Main

To the Jewish community of Pressburg

May your reverence for God add years to your lives, my beloved sacred community of Pressburg, crown among metropolises, distinguished for its reverence for God and His Torah. May God bless you out of the store of His blessing.

You have sustained me in my pursuit of Torah and sacred service since Tishre 5567 [1806] in training students in the thousands, scholars of substance who have filled the face of the world with fruitage [Isa. 27:6] and wisdom, praised be God.

I ask that you not permit the rabbinic chair to remain vacant more than two years; and do not install in it other than a recognized sage, not one who will raise his voice in preaching, but who is truly renowned for uprightness and reverence for God and for the Torah of Moses—a Ravina and Rav Ashi from childhood*—that has no traffic with heretical writings, that will not preach in the vernacular. Appoint one who will preach on rabbinic homilies; one who will not show favoritism and will accept no bribes, neither bribes of money nor bribes of honors, glory, or pride, but one who is humble, modest, and a teacher of Torah.

Thou, O God, strengthen Thy people and the people of Pressburg, in material substance, honor, and length of days in reverence of God and His Torah until the coming of the Redeemer.

*Rav Ashi and Ravina, last of the Amoraim (latter generations of Talmud scholars), who organized and edited the Gemara and arranged the Six Orders of tractates in their present order (Rashi Tractate *Baba Metzia* 86b). The intent here is to emphasize the need for a Torah prodigy.

My daughters and daughters-in-law, be extremely careful not to reveal any portion of your bodies, God forbid, by wearing shortened attire as is done today. Heaven forbid that there be anyone of this type among those reared in my household. You will certainly refrain from imitating those women who uncover their hair, and I forbid this even for a single hair, and even artificial hair. May you find favor, mercy, kindness, and compassion, and rear your children and children's children in Torah and sacred service as ordained by the Lord our God. May the Lord our God be with us and with our children forever.

Moshe Yehoshua Zelig Hakohen

Rabbi Moshe Yehoshua Zelig Hakohen (c. 1790–1855) was head of the Rabbinic Court in Ayzpute and Kuldiga, in Latvia. His will is written in the form of hanhagot, rules for daily conduct of the God-fearing, incorporating rituals, ethical behaviors, and commonsense guidelines for the conduct of one's secular affairs. In the eighty-nine items enumerated in this will we find the religious and secular rules intermingled and presented in no particular order. This suggests that the list of hanhagot was written down over a period of years, and that the writer saw no sharp distinction between sacred duties and ethical conduct. The first sixty-six of the rules appear here.

Tenth of Tevet, 5609 [January 4, 1849]

Praise unto the Creator and blessings unto Him Who creates all, Who enjoined our father Abraham to instruct his children after him that they keep the path of God. We may ask: But after that, when at the revelation of Sinai, He conveyed to us all the observances and admonitions, both the Written Law and the Oral Law which are pertinent unto the end of all time, from which there is nothing to detract and to which nothing may be added, what, then, can we say after that in instructing our children to follow the path of God, for what can we add to the Torah?

Still, I perceive it as an obligation for every individual to instruct his children, to caution them, to remind them to be alert against forgetting aught of God's will in His Torah, or these traits of the righteous:

1. To strengthen oneself to arise in the morning to the service of the Creator.

2. To cleanse the body thoroughly.

3. To recite the Torah benedictions with true devotion and to study Torah for its own sake, each according to his God-given endowments.

4. To pray with utmost devotion, as described in *Nefesh Hahayyim,* section 2, page 7.

5. To control oneself.

6. To be long-suffering—among the insulted, never the insulters; among those who are insulted but never respond in kind, even when it is by one's wife or household member.

7. If possible, to eat to somewhat less than full satiety.

8. Ceasing to eat while still desiring food is even more meritorious than *fasting*.

9. To avoid ingesting any excessive food and drink, because these excesses cause many problems, God forbid.

10. To avoid vows and oaths and all things doubtful.

11. To beware of deceit.

12. To write a will at a time when one is well and strong, in the clarity of mind, in proper order and as appropriate.

13. Prepare burial garments.

14. Avoid any sharp business transactions and whatever is contrary to the law and honesty.

15. Write down all items and subjects that require improvement either in matters of personal traits or good deeds, each according to the requirement, in order to remember it constantly and correct it with all possible speed.

16. Do not walk too straight and tall [haughtily].

17. Never worry about any worldly matter, but rather do everything in a rational way, according to the teachings of Torah.

18. Trust in God, that He will certainly do everything for your benefit— for "What is past is no more, and the future's still in store."

19. After listening to what one's fellow says, one should think through well in his own mind how to answer carefully and pleasantly ("with milk and honey") whether to answer yes or no, or to say, "I don't remember . . . I don't know . . . I forgot . . . or give me time to recall it."

Never answer what was not asked, but only to clarify according to the need. *Before* answering, one can still reply and say what he wants, but after he speaks the utterance is master over the speaker.

If one does not wish to accede to the wishes of another, let him reply in a manner of utmost courtesy.

20. Write down any and all miraculous and wondrous occurrences that happen to you.

21. Avoid doing a task that is beyond your physical strength.

22. Avoid a business transaction that appears difficult to complete successfully.

23. Do not pay before receiving the item of purchase: do not lend

money in a questionable situation except to a poor *ben Yisrael;* lend only with a pledge [collateral], but even if he fails to repay, do not foreclose on him.

24. Avoid entering into partnerships unless absolutely necessary.

25. Remove yourself from anger and pride to the utmost possible extreme.

26. Conduct yourself in the way of modesty to the utmost extent possible, as explained by the revered Shalah [Rabbi Shlomo Halevi Horowitz], p. 7, column 2: Each person whose inclination moves him to right his ways and his deeds, let him pursue humility to perfection, accept abuse but never give any, hear himself denigrated but never react, then will the Divine Presence rest upon him immediately.

27. At home wear the plainest of garments; elsewhere, respectably, and in honor of Sabbath and festival, according to one's station, the best affordable.

28. Do not think or talk about things that may bring on the slightest conceit, even in matters of Torah.

29. Throughout the weekdays keep to a minimum eating, drinking, and use of elegant utensils.

30. Never seek after luxuries, but only for absolute necessities; except for the requirements of hospitality and the needs of religious observances.

31. Fulfill "Know Him in all your dealings" [Prov. 3:6].

32. Perform your good deeds in private when possible, in order to observe the scriptural ". . . and walk humbly with your God" [Mic. 6:8].

33. Revere your father and mother in every conceivable matter.

34. If there should befall some anxiety or difficult circumstance, God forbid, immediately eliminate anguish from your heart and thoughts, and think instead how insignificant this is compared to all the troubles that are possible, God forbid. For instance, having to go begging from door to door, naked and lacking in everything; having creditors while lacking even necessities; illness; being tortured with iron instruments; being sentenced to cruel flogging; being condemned to hard labor in Siberia; having many children while the household is without food or raiment, and lacking a dwelling; and other troubles of various kinds as

have befallen some of our contemporaries. And even if, God forbid, all one's days are pain-filled or, on the contrary, if one's days are passed in rejoicing and happiness and pleasant times, let him think: What is all this worth next to the delights and benefits of eternal life in the hereafter, where it is all perfect without end? Then it will be easy to tolerate all the suffering of this world, just as it is easier to suffer the various tribulations of the journey because of the serenity and rest within his own home, because all our earthly days are like unto the shadow of a bird in flight, and one hour of pleasure in the hereafter is worth an entire lifetime in this world.

35. Have faith that the Almighty, praised be He, will do all for your benefit—everything God does is only for good.

36. Arrange all matters pertaining to both social and divine relations diligently and with utmost dispatch, in keeping with our religious law.

37. Send your children to a proper tutor, one who is God-fearing, to instruct them in Torah and in good habits to age eighteen; and if beyond that, so much the better.

38. Wed your sons to wives who are daughters of Torah scholars, and give your daughters in marriage to devout Torah scholars; give them in marriage before the age of sixteen.

39. Deal faithfully.

40. Recite all benedictions with devotion.

41. Tithe the principal, then tithe the profit; and if you wish to give double, one-fifth, then may blessings overtake you.

42. Before each daily morning worship give a half-kopek to charity. It is good to keep charity money in a separate pocket so that it is available at all times for a *mitzvah*.

43. Do everything possible to maximize the amount of time free of all concerns, both for sacred service and for the sake of limiting worldly occupation.

44. Seclude yourself for a short period every day to contemplate the ultimate purpose of man's existence in the world, and to strive with the greatest diligence possible to be fit for the service of the Creator, praised be He.

45. Remember all the good the Creator does for us despite our vexing

Him constantly; therefore we too are duty-bound to imitate His traits and act kindly even to those who vex us. But for evil do not return good, as explained in Midrash Rabba.

46. Remove yourself from anything that may lead to transgression and sin, heaven forbid.

47. Teach yourself a specific tractate or other Torah source until you know it by heart, in order to be able to study and contemplate it en route, at mealtime, in the darkness, and at work in places where it is not possible to use books. Or, at least, think always of God's name, as it is written in the *Book of the Covenant,* under Love, ". . . except in a place where it is prohibited to contemplate Torah subject matter."

48. Other than essential things, do not think or talk about subjects other than Torah matters, as written in *Nefesh Hayyim,* page 15, section 4, citing Avot D'Rabbi Nathan, "whoever keeps the words of the Torah on his heart, is exempt from ten things," etc.

49. A kilogram of bread per day and a little water are adequate for a man in good health; for raiment, linen garments or wool cloth.

50. Avoid listening to any obscene speech.

51. Keep your possessions out of sight.

52. Learn a trade that is honest and simple.

53. Do not make a halakhic ruling, even on fully familiar matters, without consulting the *Shulhan Arukh,* at least.

54. Train yourself in the habit of balance, expecting in equal amounts criticism and praise, sadness and joy, pain and pleasure. Supervise your children so they make progress in their studies; have them review what they have learned, act according to the laws of Torah and good manners. Also, oversee the members of your household and community, insofar as possible, to guide them in good and righteous paths, according to the laws of Torah.

55. If you should have a falling-out with another person, make every effort to settle it between yourselves. But if it is impossible to do so, then go before an arbitrator in good faith, without resorting to squabbles or strife, God forbid.

56. Anything we imagine to be good and proper at a given time may alter in the course of changes brought on by events. But the statutes and

judgments of the Torah, the precepts, the commandments, and the virtues in both the written and Oral Law, in the Talmud, in the Midrash, in the sacred *Zohar,* and in the responsa, all these remain true and applicable, immutable eternally without change, for ". . . the word of the Lord is tried" [2 Sam. 22:31, Ps. 18:31], so depart not from it right or left.

57. At times when not studying Torah or performing *mitzvot,* read and reread all that is written here; and your eyes will discern even more than is written in it; and may God be with you.

58. Do everything according to the will of the Creator, blessed be He, and ignore the evil inclination who blinds man, showing the light as darkness and the darkness as light, diverting him from truth, devouring his days with the vanities of the times, not having any time for thought to sacred service as is fitting and right. For these reasons I have written these brief notes, small in size but of high quality, that one can review quickly and recall, and thus escape the machinations of the evil inclination.

59. Learn a little penmanship, arithmetic, language, and the outside sciences, but do not waste too much valuable time on these trifles; and even this small amount of time should be in the privacy of your home with a good tutor who is also God-fearing. In this way you avoid the slightest calumny and heretical ideas contrary to the Torah, God forbid; and restrict your review of these [outside] studies to those places where it is forbidden to think about Torah.

60. Beware of all falsehood because "He that speaketh falsehood shall not be established before mine eyes" [Ps. 101:7]. Indeed, falsehood is the greatest *kelippa** of all, heaven forbid.

61. Hearken, my friends, my children, to the instruction of your father, and take pity upon me, yourselves, and your offspring—I enjoin you by the parental decree to observe and to perform all that is written and received in the Torah of Moses our teacher, of blessed memory; and just as it is obligatory for a child to obey his father during the father's lifetime, so is it obligatory *after* his death. As it is written in the *Zohar*

Kelippa is the "husk" which in kabbalistic thought refers to the force of evil which may overlay the force of good.

(*Behukotai*), that a child's reverence for a parent applies both during the parent's lifetime as well as afterward. Also in Midrash Rabba, Chapter 67.

You know from your youth that I have given you as many benefits as possible, so let these words be engraved in your hearts. Do not deviate from them under any circumstance, and act only in accordance with religious law; never embarrass anyone, because "he who embarrasses anyone in public loses his share in the hereafter" [Jerusalem Talmud, Tractate *Hagiga* 2:1].

Every day after my death, for the first thirty days or so, you should read this will in order to mark and perform everything in it without omission.

If you should be inclined to practice asceticism, do thus: abstain from idle talk for a day or two, according to your willpower, not allowing any idle utterance to escape your lips. This will benefit the soul more than any affliction from fasting or other afflictions, particularly in this weakened generation.

62. Don't become involved in flattery even when it seems permissible; it stupefies the feelings of a person.

63. This is a time schedule for each twenty-four-hour day:

For midnight prayers*—½ hour
Mishnah—1 hour
Pentateuch—1 hour
Cantillation—1 hour
Midrash—½ hour
Grammar—½ hour
Eyn Ya'akov—½ hour
Kabbala—½ hour
Morning prayers (public worship)—1 hour
Responsa—1 hour
Talmud—3 hours
Ethics—1 hour
Research study—½ hour
Homily—½ hour

*Over the destruction of the Temple and for the restoration of Israel.

Preparation—¹/₂ hour
Writing and arithmetic—¹/₂ hour
Bodily care—¹/₂ hour
Afternoon prayers—¹/₂ hour
Labor or business—3 hours
All meals—1 hour
Evening prayers—¹/₂ hour
Rest—¹/₂ hour
Sleep—5 hours

After this fashion everyone should divide his twenty-four-hour day, according to his concerns and needs, his energy, health, and knowledge. Probably to this the Gemara alludes when it states "Set you times for study" [*Sayings of the Fathers* 1:15], that everyone should establish regular times for daily sacred service.

64. Seclude yourself daily for a brief period to meditate and to correct whatever requires improvement in the sacred service for the purpose of which you were placed in this world.

65. Ask forgiveness from every person and be forgiving of everyone both in speech and deed, as set forth in *Bet Avraham*.

66. If you need to train yourself in a desirable trait, then practice this trait to the utmost extreme until you are habituated to it. Afterward, practice it in the normal [moderate] way, as described by Maimonides, of blessed memory.

At the end of his will, Reb Moshe Hakohen lists miraculous events in the lives of his family members. This is in keeping with the suggestion made in paragraph 20 of his will. The following are examples from his list acknowledging his debt to Providence:

These are some of the miracles and wonders I am aware of that the Almighty performed in my behalf in His great mercy and compassion:

In the year 1809 I was gravely ill, critically, and the Almighty in His compassionate mercy restored me to health after six weeks.

In 1822 my wife Rachel was ill for three weeks, and thanks to God Who healed her in His kindness.

In winter 1824 a severe, unexplained palsy afflicted my son Dov Ber in his left arm, and he recovered from it, thanks to God.

In 1825 a heavy weight struck me, and as I fell, the beam of the well fell upon me; from all this I emerged safely, praise to the Almighty's compassion.

In 1826 I suddenly had no source of income whatever, and the Almighty sent salvation through the intervention of Mr. Nahum ben Hayyim of Lebau, who established me in a respectable post in Meinegin.

On January 14, 1828, a fire broke out in the middle of the night, and praised be God, the fire extinguished itself within the hour.

In summer 1828 a large piece of plaster fell from the ceiling on my head and, thank God, it did not injure me at all.

On April 30, 1829, my four sons fell very ill, three with very high fever, and thanks to the Almighty's mercies, within six weeks they were all cured.

On May 30, 1839, I fell from the carriage and struck my head and leg on a stone and, thank the Almighty, in three days I was well.

In 1840 one of my sons suffered deliriums and the Almighty sent him healing through Physician Barr of Talesin.

On February 19, 1845, one of my daughters suffered deliriums and due to God's mercy she was restored to health in a short time, without the aid of a human healer.

On January 6, 1848, my son Solomon reported to the military authorities for military service in behalf of my family and, thank God, he was declared exempt.

On January 3, 1849, at 3:00 o'clock after midnight, the heavy wall closet fell and crushed the table and bed next to me, and it missed me by a hair's-breadth and, blessed be God and blessed be His name, I was not injured.

Benjamin M. Roth

*This unusual ethical letter (*iggeret) *was written in 1854 by Benjamin M. Roth to his son Solomon, just prior to the latter's leaving for the United States from the family home in Hechingen, Württemberg, Germany. The letter was handed to the son by his father. Solomon and his brother Moses settled in Milwaukee, and later in Cincinnati.*

Hechingen, June 1854

My Dear Son:

It is doubtful whether we shall see each other again in life; and from afar I cannot warn you against such dangers as often threaten youth. Yet even from the furthermost distance I shall think of you only with fatherly love and tenderness, and will at all times do everything in my power to help you. No sacrifice is too great for a father's love to bring willingly. In whatever situation you may find yourself, turn to me; and I will always show you that I am yours with an unending love, now and forever. Always have confidence in me. Before you give your confidence to a stranger—trust your father.

At this moment of our parting, since I can no longer be near you, let me give you the following precepts for life to take with you. Obey them, follow them, and you will never be unhappy. Whatever situations you may enter into, you will be able to take hold of yourself, to comfort yourself; and God, to Whom I pray daily for your welfare, will let it be well with you.

1. Always seek to keep your conscience clear, i.e., never commit an action which you will have to regret afterward. Think carefully about everything you contemplate doing before its execution, and consider its consequences, so that you will act only after due consideration. A sure test of a clear conscience is an unclouded temperament and a cheerful spirit. Since you have received both from nature, seek to preserve them.

2. Consider what you possess as a trust given you by God. Be thrifty with it, and seek to enlarge it in an honest manner. Consider it just as much the possession of your brothers and sisters, and therefore . . . let

no sacrifice appear too great for you. Wealth should never come to diminish your honor and your clear conscience. Also, never say in the manner of the cold Englishman or American: "Help your own self!" Instead, aid rather to the full extent of your powers every poor man and anyone who needs your help. In short, be thrifty for yourself, that you may be able to aid a suffering humanity with your wealth.

3. Never leave the religion that is yours by birth, the faith of your parents and ancestors. Neither wealth, nor friendship, nor the possibility of a brilliant career in life, nor seduction, nor even the love of a girl should move you to have the power to make you change your religion. Should you be forced, partly through circumstances, partly because of the dictates of reason, to omit the ceremonial observances, you must nevertheless under no circumstances depart from the basis of religion: "The Eternal, your God, is one, unique, single being." Reason and conviction can never force you to desert Judaism, since the Jewish religion is really the only one whose basic teachings can be brought into harmony with philosophy. Therefore desertion would be for worldly advantages, and these are never valuable enough to sacrifice the Eternal One or our conscience. I feel I must recommend this to you doubly, since you have a tendency toward frivolity which could lead you to an easier acceptance of this type of seduction.

Also, never have any contact with missionaries. You do not have enough knowledge of the Holy Scriptures. That way, you cannot engage in disputations with them; for they could easily lead you astray. Consider them therefore only as self-seeking cheats, or as ranting visionaries, as I have come to know them. And indeed in my conversations with them I frequently exhibited them as such in the presence of company, something I could do since I have studied Scripture from my childhood days. And yet even then it was a difficult task.

4. Do not become acquainted—not to mention closer relationships—with women. Be polite and well-mannered toward them; for the rest, as far as it is possible, keep your distance. Consider them like a sharp, pointed toy, with which one can play only occasionally—and then with the greatest of care. Seek to keep your heart free; guard it; and be not

seduced by the tempting, destructive speech and actions of your contemporaries. This last demands your closest attention.

Have no relations with a prostitute. Her breath is poison, her word the bite of a snake; and they are all alike. However, let me add here, in praise of Jewish womanhood, that with a few exceptions they have preserved much purer morals than the girls of other races; and they have contained themselves from selling their charms for money.

I recommend the above to you in particular as injunctions to be followed. With your fine appearance and cheerful temperament you will be exposed to many temptations and opportunities in regard to women. And I do not want to say much on this point, leaving it rather to your wisdom and unspoiled instincts. My deepest prayer is that you may guard the latter; and if it is your firm intention to remain pure, the good Lord will aid you in this task.

5. Do not trust a stranger; and certainly do not confide in him, particularly if he flatters you. In general, be reserved and discreet toward all. For many a wolf wears lamb's garments, and a true, honest friend can be recognized only after years of close acquaintance, and after he has passed many tests. But then, value him as a jewel—and a rare jewel, at that. If someone confides a secret to you, guard it; but do not make him your confidant in return. Again, this is a point which I must emphasize to you, since you are a trusting soul. But you yourself have already had experiences of this nature in your travels. Young as you are, you yourself know that men do not always mean what they say.

6. Never exhibit money or articles of value in front of a stranger, in an inn, or in any public place where strangers may be found. Even when you are with your acquaintances, do not act boastfully in regard to your possessions. On the contrary, rather claim to be poorer than you actually are. For there is no greater lure to crime than the great god Mammon; and needless bragging has brought misfortune to many a man.

7. Throughout life, whether you are in good or evil circumstances, keep your parents and your home in your mind. Guard firmly your resolution to return to them, even if only after many years (unless they are able to come to visit you). No matter when, no matter what the

circumstances surrounding you, they long for you; and they will receive you with open arms.

8. Do not try to see everything because of an overwhelming curiosity. Avoid any locations or places that threaten danger. Do not place yourself in danger through willfulness, carelessness, or excessively brave or needless action. However, be brave and determined where danger cannot be avoided, and at the critical stage, keep your presence of mind, for presence of mind has often turned away the gravest dangers, and has saved others when the danger seemed overwhelming.

9. Avoid the company of drunkards and merrymakers. Should you, by accident or because of unavoidable circumstances, find yourself in their presence, leave the room and the location they occupy. Suffer an insult rather than get into an argument with them, for such people cannot really insult a man of honor. As a general rule, let yourself be insulted rather than insult others. Be particular to avoid all quarrel and argument. Meet everyone in a polite and friendly fashion. If you believe that someone has slighted you, lock your sensitivity and your anger into your heart; and forgive the offender.

10. Avoid gambling; and seek to occupy your time with useful things. Any occupation is better and more honorable than gambling; for before one becomes aware of it, one may become an inveterate gambler. Gambling is the most destructive of vices. Much as I must criticize the excessive reading of novels, which damages one's sensibilities and the heart, and makes one weak and woman-like, if time must be killed which could be used for so many pleasant and useful occupations, such reading is preferable to gambling.

11. Be frugal and economy-minded. Save each heller as you would a gulden; for he who needlessly spends a kreutzer will never save a gulden. Seek to acquire wealth in an honest manner; and preserve it through economy. But let not this economy turn to miserliness. Be very saving in regard to your own needs, and limit your needs to the utmost. Avoid unnecessary luxuries, unless it be a matter of doing good. If you save without being miserly, no one will be able to entice you into acts of dishonor or crime.

12. Be meek and patient, and seek to acquire the character and patience of your mother. Through many years of continual suffering and pain she showed herself, in this manner, to be a true angel of patience. Be, as she was, forgiving when injustice or misfortune seeks you out; and strive in this to emulate your all-forgiving God.

13. Sunlight and moonshine are powerful lamps. But the light of your reason must eclipse them; i.e., do nothing in haste, nothing without due thought.

14. Passions are the mightiest of all tyrants. Give them one finger and they will at once take all of your body and soul. Seek, therefore, to keep free of them; and give them no opportunity to rule you.

15. Those who hate and envy us can bring much evil upon us; but the greatest evil can be brought upon us through our own soul when it walks the paths of foolishness and error. Therefore seek to avoid them in every way of life; strive to set yourself against their power.

16. Great tribulations bring us into bad habits; and once we become accustomed to a habit, it becomes second nature to us. Therefore do not learn any vices; and let no habit become a passion to you.

17. The lying tongue of viciousness can do us great damage, but our own tongue can be still worse. Therefore guard your mouth and tongue. Consider each word before it crosses your lips, for he who guards his mouth and lips is exposed to no danger. Particularly guard yourself against saying what you think during revolutionary times—no matter to which faction you belong. Do not enter into political discussions, and always remain in the background on such occasions. Live a private rather than a public life.

18. Do not count too much on the favor of a personage, whether he be highly placed or of low rank. But least of all rely on the favor of a great man. Their promises are an empty sound, their words a gust of wind. They prefer you as long as they need you; once the need is gone, they do not know you anymore.

19. Give in to necessity, and patiently bear what fate has in store for you. That which is done cannot be changed; and what has been decided on high cannot be nullified or avoided.

20. Despise and avoid the man of invectives, the calumniator, and the hypocrite. They would entice you and then use your words against you; and avoid a fool the way you would avoid a mad dog.

21. Long have I pondered, searched, and examined as to what constitutes man's true happiness. I have found only one bliss for him: virtue and fear of God. Hold fast to both of them, if you desire to attain happiness.

And thus I transmit to you, my beloved son, these rules for life. Seek to follow them. I particularly recommend to you that you seek to emulate your brother Moses and that you obey him; partly because he is your older brother, partly because he has an excellent, steadfast, and firm character. I do not censure you for the fact that big-city life and your growing up among strangers have in some ways been detrimental to you. This is the reason why you have almost discarded by now that steadfastness of spirit which you took with you from your parents' home. It remained longer in Moses, who stayed at home till he was seventeen, and whose character could therefore develop further. Really, you could not give me more pleasure than by living together peacefully and in brotherly harmony, as you could also give me no greater pain and sorrow than by not doing this. I do not doubt that both of you will follow my wishes, and in that way you will also fulfill the words of our sages [Hebrew]: "How good and how pleasant it is for brethren to live together in unity."

I assure you that my whole happiness exists in the happiness of my children. Believe me, no sacrifice would be too great for me to bring willingly if I could make you happy. It was a great inward struggle for me (and I had to conceal my feelings from you as from mother) to send you away from me while you were yet so young. But it was your firm desire—and I did not want to take it from you. For all eternity my feelings toward you will be those of the deepest love.

And with this I give you, now, my blessing; may it follow you on all your paths with the words [Hebrew]:

The angel who hath redeemed me from all evil bless thee; and let my name be named in thee, and the name of my fathers, Abraham and Isaac; and mayest thou grow into a multitude in the midst of the earth.

The Lord bless thee, and keep thee.

The Lord make His face to shine upon thee, and be gracious unto thee.

The Lord lift up His countenance upon thee, and give thee peace.

God make thee as Ephraim and Manasseh, like Moses in his humility, like Solomon in his wisdom, like Samson in his strength, like Absalom in his beauty, like Hezekiah in his righteousness, and like David in his reverence.

Mordekhai Mottel Michelsohn

Mordekhai Mottel Michelsohn (1800 – 1872), surnamed "Kalushiner" after the Polish city that was the center of his activities, was a highly accomplished man, thoroughly versed in Torah and in the complex economic and political affairs of his time. Conditions in nineteenth-century Poland were chaotic following the Third Partition (1795), administration of the country being for the most part by absentee Russian officials or their agents. Out of these conditions emerged leaders like Mordekhai Mottel Kalushiner to manage aspects of Poland's economic life, collect taxes, and often to serve as intermediaries between Jewish communities and the authorities. In the reign of Nicholas I, when Jewish boys were forcibly taken at age twelve for long-term military service (with the intent to convert them), Mordekhai Kalushiner helped restore countless boys to their families by interceding in their behalf. The text of this will is almost unique in the harshness with which the writer castigates his sons, although he forgives them their shortcomings.

"Man that is born of woman is of few days, and full of trouble" (Job 14:1). Few and troubled have been the years of my life. As a lad diseases and illness wracked me, distress and suffering from the start. From the day I reached manhood I have had no rest, no tranquility. While I have achieved success, it was only with great effort, anguish, pain, and stress that I accomplished any task. Now I have advanced in years and "It is time for the Lord to work ..." [Ps. 119:126]. Is there a man who lives forever and sees not death? Therefore listen, my children to that which I admonish you: "I have meditated on the books ..." [Dan. 9:2] and know that it is a father's religious duty to instruct his children, and that doing so is a means of perfecting the soul; and this is the meaning of Scripture, "... in order that he may instruct his children and his household after him" [Gen. 18:19].

What shall I instruct you about? If about Torah and its commandments, these things are well explained already. If your hearts are inclined toward them, you will meditate on them, obey them, observe them, and benefit from them. If not, of what use are my words? For if the teachings of Torah and the books of sainted scholars abounding in the world, permanently recorded and published, do not bear fruit for you, how can I expect to do more? You will forget both me and my words.

For all that, I shall give you some useful advice: Beware of these two vices—intoxication and lying. Both of these are vile in the eyes of God and man; they are among the most despicable of habits. "Looking upon the cup when it is red" [Prov. 23:41] leads to crooked paths seeming straight. The sages comment on this verse: "The entire world seems to him as a plain; he is viewed as a laughing-stock by all who see him and his end is to be cut off" (Talmud *Yoma* 75a).

As to lying, "He that speaketh falsehood shall not be established" [Ps. 101:7] before God, nor does anyone heed his words.

In these words are included the entire Torah and its commandments, as the sages comment on the verse, "Keep thee far from a false matter . . ." [Ex. 23:7].

Thus all your utterances on every subject, including business, should be spoken in truth.

These two traits have felled many victims. Since these are well expounded and much of Torah is based on them as fundamental to what is good and ill in life, what do I add to your knowledge about them by telling you this? I tell you this day that these are habits that I have despised during my lifetime, and that doing so has proven most effective for me (besides fulfilling the biblical admonitions regarding them) for success in commercial enterprise in our day.

Furthermore, I beseech you, be soft-spoken and let your words be few in number because "In the multitude of words there wanteth not transgression" [Prov. 10:19]; "Multiply not exceeding proud talk; let not arrogance come out of your mouth" [1 Sam. 2:3]. "For as the crackling of thorns under a pot" [Eccles. 7:6], so are the words of fools.

This too you ought to practice for your own good: Daily recite a number of *Tehillim* [Psalms]; a lesser number, with devotion, is to be preferred.

I would that you desire daily study; on days when I studied I was happy and my mind was clear in conducting all my affairs. I know this because I experienced it so.

Avoid miserliness for it is a nasty trait. They speak nonsense who maintain that stinginess leads to wealth; it doesn't work that way. On the contrary! A miser never stops trying to amass a fortune; he is dead in the midst of life. When he dies, others despoil the results of his labors.

On the other hand the generous giver gains more—he enjoys his life and bequeaths a blessing at his death. Generosity should, of course, be sensible: never for the sake of honor or recognition, but according to means and specific need. That is, as appropriate to the giver and to the beneficiary.

Never take the offensive in a quarrel; avoid disputes, but in all cases "be rather of the persecuted than of the persecutors" (Talmud *Baba Kamma* 93a). Whenever I attempted to gain the upper hand over my adversaries, even though justice was on my side, I never managed to prevail. But whenever I was the target, I prevailed over them. Also, avoid communal politics, even when you are in the right because the Evil Inclination will cast his net to deny truth and to show good as evil in accusing you. If at such times you keep your peace and do not seek to prevail, then those tidal waves will ebb as quickly as they surged.

And now, my children, obey the instruction of your father. Know that you have been rebellious for as long as I have known you. You have not been obedient and have not appreciated the benefits I have given you. Your personal conduct and your business practices have caused me vexation and pain. I was abhorrent in your eyes; my ways were not followed.

But why should I cry out against you for wrongdoing? All men are lacking in wisdom. We all are God's children, one God created us; have we not one father?* Yet though we see all the benefits that God grants us and His kindnesses to us at all times and at every hour, still we transgress. Nevertheless God, our faithful Father, in His mercies continues to spare us, forgives us, and does not withhold His kindnesses from us.

I am no more than human. I therefore forgive and pardon you; and so may God forgive you for unintended transgressions, causing them to vanish and be forgotten. Only this I entreat you: that you fulfill all that I ask with a good will; as I have instructed, so shall you do. Then will you enjoy long life and it will go well with you. Your father, Mottel Michelsohn of Kalushin.

Thus have I Directed you, my children; obey and let your souls live.

Concluded on the eve of Shabbat Nahamu, 5627 [1867], here at Kalushin.

*Transposition of Mal. 2:10.

Elias Raphael Rosenbaum

The following will appears to be unduly reproachful but may reflect only the stricter parental control typical in traditional family life of a hundred years ago. Jekutiel, the elder son, was forty-three years old at the time this will was written, and Ben Zion, twenty-eight, was in America. The family history, in The Rosenbaums of Zell: A Study of a Family, *reveals that Ben Zion left for America following an incident in which he shot and wounded a burglar. Because there was at that time an anti-Semitic wave in Germany, his father advised him to leave for America.*

Tuesday, 6th Nissan, 5641 (1881)

To my dear Family,

I am, thank God, in my seventieth year, and it might be proper to consider, being only mortal, that according to human calculations the time cannot be too far off when I also will be summoned to give account before the Almighty for my actions in this world.

In the first instance I will have to answer about the upbringing of my children, God bless them. However much I would like to believe that I have fulfilled my duty, I cannot set my mind at rest in this respect as, to my greatest regret, I must confess that I am not wholly satisfied with the result so far achieved.

Therefore I turn first to my dear son Jekutiel with this serious warning. I address you as our Father Jacob did: Jekutiel, "you are my firstborn, my might and the beginning of my strength" (Gen. 49:3). You should set an example for your brother and sisters.

With an aching heart I am now turning to you, my dear Ben Zion. You have given us so much, so very much sorrow, and you have thus far unfortunately gone astray, away from the family. If, after your father's death, you are willing to do something for him, who is so deeply distressed about you—and for yourself, to atone for your great guilt—repent and do *Teshuvah* [repentance]. The first step of repentance is to regret all your mistakes, and to cease doing them. You have to be strictly fair and honest, and under no circumstances let an untrue word pass your lips. I know that with such deeply rooted corruption the return is difficult. However, think of the seriousness of your iniquities and try to return, because nothing can withstand against a person who repents. If you will seriously change your ways, all I have told your brother will also apply to you, and I will gladly pardon you if you fulfill your duties.

The son, Ben Zion, appears to have taken his father's words to heart, as is evident from one of the codicils to the main part of the father's will.

Monday, 7th Adar, 5642 (1882)

I thank God infinitely that he gave me the *zehiah* [privilege] that you, my dear son Ben Zion, have returned already during my lifetime, and are leading a religious life in America; and I am pardoning you full-heartedly for everything of the past. God will give you the strength to live by His holy will, and will make you happy; and you will endeavor to establish the good name of the family also in the distant country. You will therefore do for your father as far as possible that which I have mentioned before.

Nathan Marcus Adler

Rabbi Nathan Marcus Adler (1803 – 1890) served as chief rabbi of the British Empire from 1844 to 1890. His leadership was a major factor in the establishment of Jews' College in 1855, and he led the Jewish community in Great Britain to develop many of its modern characteristics.

December 31, 5644 – 1883.

I have been very ill, and near death, but Almighty God in His mercy has so far restored me to health that I am able, although inadequately, to write. Being in Brighton, and no longer surrounded by the members of my family and able to speak to them, I feel bound to lay the following religious duties to the hearts of my children, grand: and great-grandchildren, with the earnest wish that they may always observe them, and thereby keep my memory fresh and green. If in the following admonitions I speak less of the so-called moral duties, do not for a moment think that I consider moral duties of less importance than religious duties. Such is not the case. They also are the Commandments of the Lord—as sacred and as binding as the religious duties. My reason is because in our times there is greater laxity with regard to religious duties, and more temptation to neglect them.

The main principle of Judaism is the Lord's command (Deut. 6:3), "And thou shalt love the Lord thy God with all thy heart, and with all thy soul, and with all thy might."

In those words the Lord enjoined us to love the great Creator of the universe and the Disposer of our life with all our heart, all our feelings and emotions, hopes and aspirations; to worship Him in awe and reverence, to submit to His ruling Providence in joy and sorrow, gladness and suffering, amid plenty and in need, and especially to restrain our passions. We shall love the Lord with all our soul, with the spiritual, rational, and immortal part of our nature. We shall try to know, understand, and mentally grasp the doctrines of our religion, so that when the results of science seem to clash with our religious convictions, we shall not allow them to disquiet our mind, but consider that our faith is based on reason, and that in Judaism religion and science are not incompatible, their hostility being but apparent. The word *nafshekha* implies also life, as our sages explain *"afilu notel et nafshekha."* We should love our God with all our life, with our whole existence, so that we should regard our religion higher than our life; and like our fathers and mothers of old, rather give up our life than forsake our religion. And, last, we should love God with all our might. We are bound to show the warmth of our heart, the strength of our convictions, by the very performance of the Laws of our God. The mainspring, the very touchstone of the worth of our love toward God, consists in our carrying out the obligations we owe to Him, to ourselves, and to our neighbors, with all energy, courage, fervor, and affection, unmindful of the difficulties, annoyances, or sacrifices by which the duties are sometimes accompanied. Therefore the command is *ushemartem va'asitem* (Lev. 19:37, 4:6), "Ye shall keep (my ordinances) and do them."

 These Laws are declared first in the Torah, the five books of Moses, the greatest of all prophets, through whom the Law was revealed. They are also contained in the *Neviim,* the prophets, who were inspired by God, and bound to promulgate His will; and, last, in the *Ketuvim,* the writings of holy men who were inspired by God, but not bound to promulgate their inspirations. These twenty-four books form our Holy Bible. We have to regard the Bible as our most precious book, not alone because it affords us guidance through life, but because it teaches Israel his origin, his history, his mission to influence mankind in the knowledge of the only one God, and his sublime calling to bring about the time of the Messiah, when every knee shall bow and every tongue swear fidelity to our God, when He will be one and His name one.

Stimulate, therefore, my dear ones, your children to read every day in the morning, after prayers, or at some other suitable time, one chapter of the Bible, so that it may be impressed upon their memory.

These Laws are expounded and illlustrated by the rabbis in the *Torah sheb'al peh* or Oral Law. This teaches the manner and the mode how the written laws must be carried out. It is also called tradition, because it is an explanation of our laws which has been transmitted to us from generation to generation, from the very time that they were first proclaimed. The necessity for such explanation is evident, e.g.:

The Torah commands (Deut. 6:8), "Thou shalt bind them (those words) for a sign on thy hand, and they shall be as frontlets between thine eyes, and thou shalt write them upon the doorposts of thy house." Without the Oral Law we should not know how the words should be bound on our hands, or as frontlets between our eyes, or how they should be written on the doorpost of our house. All the festivals are appointed to be kept on certain days of the month. Without the Oral Law we should not know which month is meant, when it commences, or at what period of the year. We should not know the various ordinances of the festivals, the precepts of tefillin and *mezuzah*, the regulations as to inheritance, and several others. Read, therefore, my beloved, every Sabbath the Sedrah in Hebrew, with the Targum or an easy Commentary, or if not sufficiently conversant with Hebrew, read it in English, and make yourselves acquainted, at least on Sabbath, with the rabbinical literature.

Home, however, a Jewish home, forms the center of the divine Laws. It is in their house that husband and wife must live in peace and domestic happiness, under all the vicissitudes, the sunshine and cloud of their life. It is here where father and mother must train their children with parental love and solicitude, receiving filial love and affection in return. It is here where parents must educate their children in our holy religion, educate more by example than by words and lessons. Here parents must observe the dietary laws with all rigor, and teach their children to keep those tenets as strictly out of doors. Here the wife must take care that nothing *trefa* come into her premises, nor be ashamed to look to her kitchen, taking care that her servants observe everything religiously, and especially that they separate meat from milk.

Do not listen, my dear children, as regards the Law "Thou shalt not seethe a kid in its mother's milk" [Ex. 23:19, 34:26; Deut. 14:21], to the criticism of the so-called Neologians, who assert that the Law must be taken literally, for this would be senseless. Depend upon it, from the very time of its first promulgation it was expounded and carried out in its extended sense. Depend upon it, its repetition three times in the Torah should teach us to keep the Law most scrupulously, neither to cook a mixture of meat and milk, nor to eat, nor to use it. Besides, the Law belongs to those ordinances of which we do not know exactly the reason, whether it be spiritual, moral, or sanitary, or all three together; but this we know, the divine Lawgiver gave us no precept without some beneficent motive.

I need not lay to your hearts the importance of fulfilling your duty during the week, in whatever your calling may require. It consists especially in industry, unflagging diligence in your employment, whether it be business or profession. This industry must be accompanied by strict integrity, not only in large, but even in smallest matters; not only toward your co-religionists, but toward non-Israelites. This integrity will obtain for you a good name, and reputation, but what is of greater value, it will conduce to the sanctification of the Lord, which the Lawgiver called *kiddush ha-Shem*. Whatever your calling, shun, oh, my dear ones, every kind of usury, for usury still constitutes, alas! the malignant canker which sullies the fair fame of our nation.

As it is your duty to be industrious during the work days, so you are bidden to repose and rest from all kind of work on the Sabbath. The Sabbath teaches the great truths of Judaism. Sabbath has been the cause and moving spirit of Israel's preservation during the centuries of its persecution. Let it be such to you—a day of joy, of tranquility from care, and of rejoicing. Distinguish it by a better meal, better raiment, by exercise in the free air, but above all by a higher rest, a rest that sanctifies the name of the Lord, by greater devotion to, and at, public worship, by more zealous study of the Torah, especially by the examination of your children, and ascertaining how far they have advanced in their Hebrew knowledge. Keep the day holy, the whole day, from the beginning of the Sabbath to its end. Avoid any business, writing, or riding after the Sabbath has commenced, however early in the day it might appear to you. The Friday afternoon, when Sabbath has commenced, is as sacred as the middle of the day. Forget not the words of Nehemiah (13: 15 – 23) that the profanation of the first hour of the Sabbath brought evil on our forefathers.

If you lead a pious life you will escape the punishment against which the Lord has warned the sinner, and you will partake of the choice blessings the Lord has promised to the individual and the nation. You will enjoy in this world the cheering consciousness of having followed the supreme direction of your God. And hereafter, when your heart ceases to beat and your flesh faileth, there will abide forever the soul that is spirit of God's spirit, your eternal portion that will live forever, that will be satisfied with fullness of joy in the Lord's presence, pleasures—*sova semahot biminkha netzah*—forevermore! [Ps. 16:11].

Most solemnly I entreat all my sons and daughters, sons- and daughters-in-law, grand- and great-grandchildren, to be good Jews and Jewesses, regardful of future reward and punishment, to lead a life of firm morality and strict observance of our Laws in their household and in the education of their children, to become and to continue patterns to others by their benevolent actions, and God's choicest blessings will accompany them!

Isaac Elhanan Spektor

"Reb Yitzhak Elhanan" (1817 – 1896), the eminent rabbi of Kovno, Lithuania, was one of the most beloved of leaders in modern times. A ranking authority on the Law, he did much to alleviate the tragic plight of agunot. *He was tireless in organizing help for stricken European communities, providing religious aid and guidance to Jews in Argentina, the United States, and elsewhere, and strove always to better the lot of Jewish soldiers in the Russian army. An early supporter of* Hovevei Zion, *he publicly advocated settlement in Eretz Yisrael as a religious duty. Reb Yitzhak Elhanan was universally recognized for his great erudition and he was beloved for his open-mindedness and genial manner. Institutions have been named for him in Europe and in America, including the Rabbi Isaac Elhanan Theological Seminary in New York.*

With the help of God, blessed be He,
Heshvan 9, 5649 [October 14, 1888], Kovno

To my esteemed, sacred congregation of Kovno, may you flourish.

. . . As it is the duty of each individual to enjoin his sons and all who are close and obedient to him to keep to the way of God, that is, His Torah . . . and because of my great love, the love of a father for his children, which I feel for the members of my sacred congregation in whose midst I have dwelled and served as rabbi these twenty-six years, I see it as my responsibility to leave my will as a benefit and benediction for all the members of the sacred congregation.

1. From the depths of my heart I give thanks and appreciation and blessings for all things good to the entire holy congregation as one, to the various groups, collectively and individually, for all the benefits they bestowed upon me, for maintaining a center for Torah. For it was here in your distinguished community I was privileged to promulgate most of my Torah studies, and I was treated with honor in your midst. May God reward you for your deeds, and may your reward be complete at His hand, blessed be He.

2. I entreat the beloved members of my community to be strong in God's Torah and in the observance of His precepts, in particular to be careful about Sabbath observance and to avoid desecrating the Sabbath

... to train up your children in the paths of Torah, never letting them depart, God forbid, from the study of Mishnah and Gemara, the principles and foundations of the holy Torah. Similarly, to rear them and educate them morally and ethically according to the ways of Torah.

3. I implore you to preserve peace among yourselves, to seek peace and to pursue peace, as it is written, "seek peace and pursue it" [Ps. 34:15]. It is well known to you how much I strove with all my might for the sake of peace.

4. Similarly, you know something of the great efforts I have put forth, with the help of God, even in the most difficult times, to enhance Torah and to increase the numbers of those who study it. And you have merited becoming a center of Torah with a multitude of scholars. I beg of you to stand firmly on behalf of Torah scholars in the manner I myself publicly espoused, with God's help, by self-sacrifice and without heed to my waning strength during my older years; and may the merit of Torah for the multitudes stand you and your descendants in good stead forever.

5. Strenuous were the labors I expended in efforts to provide kosher food for our Jewish brethren serving in the armed forces. I plead with you in the strongest terms, excellencies, to put forth ever-stronger efforts and increased vigor, with God's help, toward this precious cause.

6. According to Jewish law, my son Zvi Hirsh, may he flourish, is entitled to my rabbinic post, and indeed he has represented me in all matters. But besides the right he has by law, he is also highly qualified and worthy of this position; I therefore have confidence that you will install him in the rabbinical post. . . . and I hereby forgive and pardon with full pardon and forgiveness all who provoked or vexed me with deed or word, and bless this entire holy community out of the depths of my heart and soul; and I beg that, just as I forgive and pardon them and forgo my own feelings for the sufferings of love I experienced on many occasions over a variety of matters, so may they, from their side, act with kindness and compassion toward my son, rabbi and presiding judge of the Rabbinic Court, may he flourish; and by virtue of setting aside their opposition, in deference to his knowledge of Torah and his piety, this peace will serve as an instrumentality of blessing for him and for your excellencies alike. Similarly, I ask of the entire holy community, may

they flourish, if perchance I injured any among them monetarily or through some slight or other involvement, that they forgive me just as I forgive all of them.

7. My closing words I end with a prayer and a benediction offered to the Almighty, blessed be He, in behalf of the entire sacred congregation to which I ministered in the office of the rabbinate these many years, and I bless you: Blessed are you to God; may God guard you from every calamity and affliction; may He bestow upon you abundant blessing and deliverance and grant you a life of peace, prosperity, and honor, reverence for heaven and love of Torah; and may He fulfill all the desires of your heart for good.

I am your faithful friend and servant who writes tearfully and who hopes that you will fulfill all the cherished matters stated above, that it may be counted to your great merit forever, and that you may be blessed many times over because of it. Amen, so may it be.

> My signature herewith,
> Yitzhak Elhanan ben Harav Hatzadik
> Rabbi Israel Isser, of blessed memory
> Residing here, Kovno

Isaac Komiansky

Ethical wills frequently allude to key events in the lives of their writers in order to illustrate or emphasize an instructive point. Seldom is a detailed history part of the traditional testament as it is in the case of the autobiographical ethical will of Isaac Komiansky (1828 – 1903). But the story of the writer's life (abridged here) is not related to his children to serve merely as a personal odyssey but as the medium in which were cultivated his truest convictions and ethical perspectives. Of further interest is the fact that this testament was published in Kiev, in 1911, as a small book containing both Hebrew and Russian versions.

July 26, 1888

To my beloved children: I set before you this day these words as a memorial.

Fixed are man's years on earth, determined are his days of travail. Yet no man knows his span, like fish held fast in the net. I have therefore decided to search my heart to consider my lifetime and all my labor under the sun to this day; to describe all this and relate to my children all the troubles that have overtaken me during the years of my life. At the time, each of the troubles delivered a hammer-blow to my head. But now, with the passage of time, I regard them as vain trifles one and all. They are all gone now, like a dream that has fled, leaving no trace.

Indeed, a contemplative man understands that one need not be overwhelmed by human failure any more than by some success that he may experience. For time erases everything; and in the course of years all is borne away on the wind, forgotten. All but the loving-kindness of the Almighty, Who sustains us in life and puts no stumbling blocks before our feet, Whom we praise eternally both for the good He bestows on us and for the ills which befall us during our lifetimes, and which we have survived.

Let me enumerate for you, my dear children, the obstacles which fate has strewn in my path at various times, each of which was burdensome in relation to my circumstances at the time.

In the summer of 1847 I journeyed with my father-in-law to the fair at Romen, and in my first transaction I lost my entire dowry. My late father then took us in to his house in Moghilev where I stayed for several years with my wife; our son Ya'akov was born there. My parents provided for all our needs while I studied diligently.

After several years, I began working with the renowned Isaac Monastiricher in Smolensk, then in summer and winter 1852 in Brisk. Some years later I went into the sugar business with Moghilev people. In Vitebsk we had a large sugar warehouse and in spring 1861 the warehouse burned, and it was not insured. My share of the loss cost me a substantial part of my worth.

Later I went to work managing Sa'adia Schure's sugar business in Kiev, while my wife stayed in Moghilev. I stayed with him for about ten years. During that time I made some successful investments and in winter 1871 the price of sugar went up. In the course of a three-month period I earned 25,000 rubles!

But in 1872 tragedy struck. My beloved son Ozer was stricken with consumption, and in summer they brought him to Kiev. The physicians gave no hope for his recovery and advised that he be taken to Meran. My wife took him to Meran where he died that winter. That tragedy caused me such grief that its effects are with me to this day.

Later (in 1882) my son Ya'akov came to Kiev and we increased our investments in sugar. Within a two-and-a-half-year period my share alone was worth 150,000 rubles, not to mention a house in Moghilev, while my sons Ya'akov, Moshe, and Leib had their own substantial sums. But then the entire sugar market turned upside down, and all the transactions we undertook resulted only in great losses. I lost everything and even went into debt. Still, I do not despair; the loving-kindness of the Almighty is not exhausted. I continue to hope to God that the sunlight of success will shine upon me, for His saving power can come in the blink of an eye. . . . The clouds will disperse and the sun will shine, bringing light, joy, and splendor. . . .

3. Observe, my dear children, the changes that occurred over the years and see whether we ought to become so excited when success shines on us or, God forbid, the opposite. For man's life is woven alternately of good times and bad. Therefore in good times one must learn to think, wealth is not forever, there may come unwanted days of

change and darkness. And in days of trouble one must strengthen himself with trust in the Almighty, that better days will come with change for good and light. In successful times one must not become overbearing because of his wealth nor luxuriate excessively; and similarly a Jew is duty-bound to trust in God when troubles overtake him.

4. Hearken, my children, and I shall instruct you, and may God be with you. First, always cultivate the virtue of contentment, avoid excessive wants and extravagance. For extravagance is "a root that beareth gall and wormwood. . ." [Deut. 29:17]. Even when the sun of success shines upon you, beware of increasing your expenditures and those of your household. As such times you should think that perhaps days of change will come, so always manage your households at some moderate level. For while miserliness is indecent, even more disgraceful and dangerous is the vice of extravagance. Each person is obliged to secure his wealth and not squander it on vanities that benefit neither body nor soul.

5. Second, always try to be pleasant to other people. This is the way to earn the consideration of others: "Receive everyone with a cheerful countenance" [*Ethics of the Fathers,* I, 15]. Respect each person as a human being, for ". . . who is to be honored? He who honors others!" [*Ethics of the Fathers,* IV, 1]. Above all, control yourselves against ever speaking harshly to any individual. To make it easier to achieve this control, do this: think of your own imperfections and of some virtue in the other. By so doing you will avoid any coarse expression and retain self-control. And if you maintain self-control, you will surely be able to avoid these three most serious of vices: envy, ambition, and anger, which undermine body and soul and remove the individual from the world. In this way you will be loved and be a delight to God and man, happy here and hereafter.

6. Let me tell you, dear children, that I have always made it a goal to implant in my heart a love for fellowman, to respect every human being and reject arrogance and envy. I shall not delude myself to claim that I have altogether achieved this goal. Understandably, it is a great task for a plain man like myself to develop a refined spiritual quality, inasmuch as ". . . sin coucheth at the door" [Gen. 4:7], and each time a man attains some good idea or desirable thought after much contemplation, some

opposing ideas and foreign thoughts intrude that are contrary to the others. A special spiritual strength is needed for this struggle. But this I will tell you: I have always endeavored to do battle with my lower impulses, and at times I have succeeded, with God's help, to come nearer to these virtues, to overcome my inclinations by the means I have described.

You too should be able to achieve this, to habituate yourselves to leave the vices and approach the virtues mentioned. If you do so, and fulfill whatever possible of all that I ask of you and advise you to do, I will consider myself happy and successful. For this is my sole reward for all my labors—to have children who try to live righteous lives, walking in good and straight paths, finding favor in the sight of God.

7. Having alerted you to the duty of respecting all creatures and to love all men because of their humanity, it is unnecessary to caution you about loving your own brothers and sisters. For if we feel how disgraceful it is to lord it over others, how much more repellent for one to do so toward his own flesh and blood! Such a person is not truly civilized.

Necessity forces me not to remain silent about this matter but rather to speak to you about it; but a portion of my words I address expressly to the attention of my son Ya'akov:

You, Ya'akov have departed from the virtue of contentment; you have excessive ambition and arrogance. You do possess some fine qualities: you love to give of your substance to others, you are ever prepared to help and benefit other people both through deeds of personal service and monetarily as well, and often you do more than you can, such as at times when you are financially pressed. But I have seen, and it has deeply vexed me, that when your own brothers need your assistance, you withhold your hand. You also love to boast and act arrogantly toward your brothers, and act stubbornly when they are in straits. Now, at this hour, when all my thoughts are on preparing myself for the hereafter, I cannot restrain myself from raising my voice in rebuke, and to ask you, to command you, to cease acting in this manner. You must strengthen yourself and try to change your ways. I pray to the Almighty to send His help from on high to each of you out of the bounty of His hand, for all your needs throughout life; may you never be obliged to turn to one another or to outsiders. Amen.

Shmuel Tefilinsky

Among the Torah sages of twentieth-century Jerusalem, Reb Shmuel Tefilinsky (1888–1945) was one of the most highly respected. Born in Jerusalem, he left the precincts of the Old City only two or three times during his lifetime; one of those occasions is mentioned in his will. He was recognized in Jerusalem for piety, devotion to Torah, and profound talmudic scholarship. As a ben Torah, *or* ben yeshiva, *his entire life was spent in the ceaseless toil of learning and teaching Torah.*

The term ben Torah *(pl.* bnei Torah*) requires elucidation if the will of Reb Shmuel is to be understood. In every generation there have been Jews who were drawn to Torah study as their sole calling. Jewish tradition encourages other Jews to provide support for these* bnei Torah *(scholars). The sustenance thus gained was quite meager despite the relatively small number of these* bnei Torah; *but it must be remembered that the lot of the average Jew in the Old World was one of grinding poverty. Reverence for the sacred lore and for the scholars who devoted their lives to its maintenance impelled them to contribute what they could to* ezras Torah *("maintaining Torah").*

bnei Torah, *as a rule, pursued their studies under the auspices of an institution—a yeshiva (hence,* ben yeshiva*) or* kolel—*which allocated stipends to the scholars. In his will the author urges his sons, should they elect to follow his vocation, to avoid appealing to the institutional leaders for added sums. Basing himself always on appropriate traditions and verses, he suggests also that* bnei Torah *view themselves as the spiritual heirs of the Levites of old, consecrated to learning and teaching, eschewing all worldly occupations.*

The ethical will of Reb Shmuel Tefilinsky is designed as a practical guide for his children, whether or not they choose the life of the ben Torah. *The will is divided into ten sections: faith in God, maximizing learning, fixing times for study, methods of study,* musar *learning, educating sons and daughters, avoiding books known to be heretical, tithing incomes, and general rules of conduct. Excerpts from the third section are presented here.*

III. Minimize Business and Engage in Torah

1. Endeavor to the utmost to cleave to God's teachings day and night, to devote yourselves all the days of your life to Torah and to the service of God, and to labor in the Torah in order to perceive and understand, to hearken, to learn and teach and to "cast your burden on the Lord and he will sustain you" [Ps. 55:23] in the manner of the tribe of Levi. These are

the words of Maimonides, of blessed memory, Chapter 13 in the Laws of Fallow Year and Jubilee: "Why were the Levites not allotted land in Eretz Yisrael or a share in its booty along with their brethren? Because they were singled out to serve the Lord and minister to Him, to teach His upright ways and just laws to many people, as it is written: 'They shall teach Jacob Thine ordinances, and Israel Thy law. . .' [Deut. 33:10]. For this reason, they were separated from worldly affairs; they fought no battles like the rest of Israel; they inherited no land; they won nothing by means of their physical ability. They are indeed the Lord's army, as it is written: 'Bless, O Lord, his substance' [Deut. 33:11]. He, blessed be He, has won them for Himself, as it is written: 'I am your portion and your share' [Num. 18:20]."

Not only the tribe of Levi, but each well-informed, thinking person whose spirit moves him to devote himself to the service of the Lord, to know the Lord, and has walked uprightly after casting off his neck the yoke of many a cunning wile that men contrived, is indeed divinely consecrated, and the Lord will forever and ever be his portion. God will provide sufficiently for his needs, as He did for the priests and the Levites. David, may he rest in peace, declared: "The Lord is my allotted portion and my cup; thou maintainest my lot" [Ps. 16:5].

2. If it should be your lot to be among the students of the academy and to receive an institutional stipend as customary here in Jerusalem, you should consider and understand what the nature of such a stipend is, what the nature of a Torah academician is, and what is the essence of the ideal of establishing Torah academies [*yeshivot*] in Jerusalem.

Now many believe, mistakenly, that the *yeshivot* were established as a form of support for the impoverished *bnei Torah* who have no occupational skill with which to sustain themselves and their families. [They think] that if *bnei Torah* succeeded in finding a position or an occupation, they prefer to accept it and set aside their full-time Torah study for part-time, albeit regular, Torah study and avoid benefiting from alms and burdening the community. Thus the term *ben Torah* is seen in the public mind as synonymous with a poor, unskilled individual unsuited for any trade or business. Therefore, they believe, he and his wife and children are forced to live depressed, deprived lives, and it is thus a *mitzvah* to ease his pitiable condition and support him after the manner of charity.

Actually, this perception has an ugly taint to it that smacks of irreligiosity; only those remote from learning, who have no conception about Torah and its worth, entertain such notions and view *bnei Torah* as helpless idlers.

In truth, it is not so. If these "idlers" chose to engage in mundane enterprise, they would prove sufficiently alert and competent for every sort of activity; they are as equipped and capable as any in the market-place, perhaps more so, for every occupation and calling you can name, as proven by experience.

For the genuine concept of *ben yeshiva* and the basis of the idea of establishing the Torah academies is altogether different, because: there is no people who exists without a law and there can be no Jewish people without its Torah and without its teachers and leaders. Every group and every community needs people steeped in Torah to influence and teach the people the course of life and action based on the Torah, the central pillar of Judaism and the basis of its survival.

Experience has taught that in every land, city, or community where there are *yeshivot* and Torah scholars, there Judaism is at a high level, the place is suffused with the spirit of Torah, and Jewish life is strong there. In lands where *yeshivot* are lacking, Judaism is at a low level, the condition of Jewish life and faith deteriorates day by day, and the Torah is almost forgotten there, along with Jewish identity.

But, thank God, "Israel is not widowed" [Jer. 51:5], and in every time and place there still are noble spirits, dedicated and pure, whose souls yearn for the Torah and for whom all worldly attractions are as nothing compared to the delight of Torah. For them it is easy to turn their backs on all the attractions of this world. The most meager of necessities are adequate for them and they are content to live at the extreme poverty level so long as they can find space in the confines of Torah and enjoy the majestic radiance of Torah, day and night. Whenever a Torah study center is set up anywhere at all, it immediately attracts those special individuals who thirst for God's word and who come to drink from the wellsprings of Torah.

It is precisely for this ideal that Torah centers and institutions are established among our people—to provide insofar as possible for the needs of those who wish to commit their lives to study of Torah and whose spiritual existence is dependent on its pursuit. Ensuring the survival of these people and their families underlies the idea of a yeshiva. This also defines the concept of a true *ben yeshiva,* who cannot be lured even by a thousand thousand denarie of gold [*Avot* 6:9] from his Torah study, his reason for being and the sole aspiration of his life.

It follows from this that the stipend provided by the yeshiva as well as means from other sources given to the *bnei yeshiva* are not to be viewed simply as alms to the poor, but rather in the same category as gifts to the priestly and levitical classes. For the Torah placed a duty on all the other tribes of Israel to dedicate a portion of their possessions and incomes to the support of one of the tribes, this being the tribe of Levi. This tribe was specifically designated and dedicated to the service of God and to teaching all the people His straight paths and His just laws, as it is written: "They shall teach Jacob Thine ordinances, and Israel Thy law . . ." [Deut. 33:10].

So, my children, there may be among you any who yearns for and seeks to enter upon the threshold of Torah and desires to dwell in the house of the Lord all the days of his life, "to behold the graciousness of the Lord, and to visit early in His temple" [Ps. 27:4] and attain to the Crown of Torah. If so, let him ponder the decision whether he earnestly and truly wishes to assume the yoke of Torah and cast behind him all worldly treasures. If he is willing to follow the course of Torah even as described by the sages [*Avot* 6:4], "a morsel of bread with salt thou shalt eat and water by measure thou shalt drink . . ." then the joy of the Lord is your strength and true glory can follow. Furthermore, "Whoever takes upon himself the yoke of the Torah, they remove from him the yoke of government and the yoke of worldly concerns" [*Avot* 3:5].

Let this principle be engraved on your souls, in every aspect of your lives: that the purpose and rationale of study for the *ben Torah* is *not* to earn the stipend and support of the academy, as many think. On the contrary, the academy's support makes possible the study and preservation of Torah, since "without flour [i.e., basic necessities] there can be no Torah" [*Avot* 3:17].

3. Now, my sons, whoever among you will choose to enter the divine service, dedicated to God's Torah and to His word, and seeks to be counted among the hosts of the Almighty, blessed be He, then he must carefully consider and realize the significance of the sacred role he takes upon himself. He must be ever alert, constant, and courageous in his Torah pursuit. In terms of *time*, he must keep to a maximum the time at the academy, day and night; guard each moment of time to avoid wasting a single minute on extraneous matters, like a day laborer at his tasks. In terms of *achievement,* he must enhance and add to his skill in the realm of Torah knowledge through continual review until it is thoroughly mastered; and he must labor and struggle with all his might to penetrate the depths of the law, to discern the basis and reason of each issue, "to search out through debate, then arrive at conclusions in keeping with the tradition" (*Sota* 21a).

So, according to the above, the concept of *ben yeshiva* does not mean merely that one is unoccupied and whose time is his own to do with as he will, but rather he is one whose sole occupation is study of and labor in Torah. Therefore the *ben Torah* must arrange his life and his schedule of study in the very same way the businessman arranges his. Thus, for example, if he happens to be invited to a meeting, a feast, a celebration, or the like, he must consider how a storekeeper or a day worker would respond to it. Should he close his business, should he put aside his day's work for this activity and attend the event or not? For we too are "laborers hired by the day," so how are we to put down our work, our sacred service, to spend time on other things, especially on optional matters. So it is also regarding caring for children and assisting in household matters. But it is even true about seeking out good works to perform; everything requires careful deliberation and even consultation with a sage as to whether a given function is worth setting aside one's study. In any case, never regard such a matter lightly.

4. One further detail must be kept in mind seriously even though one is a *ben Torah* already fully devoted to Torah learning. That is, let him not forget at appropriate times the duty of *every* Israelite to set times for Torah study. For there are times and seasons when one is especially burdened, like the eves of festivals, ritual celebrations, or on journeys

away from home and from studies for a period of time. At such times let his attention not be diverted from the duty of setting specified times for Torah study, several hours during the day or at night. Let him not think for an instant that a *ben yeshiva* is exempt from setting aside definite times for study. For on the occasions when he cannot meditate on the Torah the entire day, he is no less duty-bound to pursue Torah than any other Jew. This feeling I first had during the World War in 1915 when there was a locust plague. The government required everyone to assist in eliminating the locusts. All of us *bnei yeshiva* traveled to the settlements in Judea, to the vineyards and orchards of the area, where we spent entire days exterminating the locusts. At that time I called it to the attention of my group that we are not exempt from setting times for Torah study.

Shalom Ansky

Shalom Ansky (1865 – 1920) is the pen name of Shlomo Zangwill Rapoport. He is most widely known as the author of The Dybbuk. *Most of his career, however, was devoted to ethnographic research, particularly in the field of Jewish folklore. Ansky, who wrote in both Yiddish and Russian, organized ethnographic expeditions in Russian and Galician cities; it is to the materials gathered during these studies that he makes reference in his will. Not mentioned in the will is the fact that Ansky gave a portion of the data collected to Yehuda Leib Peretz for his book* Mipi Ha'am.

With sound mind and clear memory, I hereby express my will regarding the inheritance I leave behind me, after my death. . . .

Besides whatever is in my flat—there are other belongings, manuscripts in St. Petersburg, Moscow, and Kiev—there are also written materials I gathered and museum items belonging to the Baron Hertz Ginzburg Jewish-Ethnographic Expedition. I attach herewith a detailed list of all items that are in the above cities, including a receipt from the Alexander III Museum for the three trunks full of museum items which I conveyed to them for safekeeping.

It is my fervent wish that anything I wrote having more or less abiding value be published in volumes, like my selected works in Yiddish and Hebrew. If it cannot be realized while I live, I turn to my friends, Ch. N. Bialik and Sh. Niger, with the request that they undertake the task of editing the publication, to take pains to see to it that my request is fulfilled.

The second part of my estate, the monetary, I bequeath in equal parts: to the Jewish Society for History and Ethnography in Vilna, to the Jewish Society for History and Ethnography in St. Petersburg, and to some similar institution for ethnography or archeology in Jerusalem (or elsewhere in Eretz Yisrael). If the [Jewish] Society for History and Ethnography in St. Petersburg is not functioning at the time of my bequest and if there is no likelihood that it will resume functioning within a period of two years, then its share shall pass to the two above-named institutions. The sums in the bequests are to serve the above institutions, first and foremost, for publishing the ethnographic materials which I assembled. The balance may be used for gathering new ethnographic data or for the purchase of objects for Jewish museums.

All the letters that are in my possession I request be conveyed to Sh. Niger or Ch. N. Bialik. If part of them appear in print and earn an author's commission, I ask that it be added to the principal of the estate. Letters to me as well as my letters [to others] that may be brought together I would very much wish to have published, edited in a manner that will carefully omit any reference to intimate incidents, particularly those that may hurt or embarrass those to whom they refer.

During the difficult years of my life, I borrowed money which I never repaid to my debtors; some of them I recall and I have a list of their names and request that they be repaid. Of the remaining ones I beg forgiveness.

I ask that no eulogies be delivered over my grave; let one of my friends recite the kaddish and read a short biography—facts only— about how I lived my life.

I beg forgiveness of anyone whom I caused pain, insult, or injury during my lifetime.

Valentin Wolff

Valentin Wolff was born in Essingen, near Landau (Rheinpfalz), in West Germany, on August 28, 1838. He died in Landau on June 16, 1924. The daughter Rosa (Mayer), mentioned in the will, immigrated to the United States from Germany in 1937 with her family.

[Not dated; written in 1924]

Today, on Sabbath Eve, I write this, feeling that my days and hours are numbered. First of all, I thank dear God, that He has granted me long life, though I have experienced both good and bad days.

Dear children and grandchild, I thank you heartily for the affection you have shown me even into my old age; may the good Lord reward you all for it. Maintain your friendship together the same as though I were still in your midst.

Especially do I thank my beloved Rosa for her devoted efforts; may better days return. Keep God before your eyes in all that you do, and be not Godless as so many are. Then will dear God keep you in His protection and enable you to experience only good.

Your still-living father and grandfather.

Hayyim Elazar Shapira
(The Munkatcher Rebbe)

Reb Hayyim Elazar Shapira (1869–1937) was the official rabbi of the city of Munkatch (till World War I in Hungary, then Czechoslovakia) and the surrounding communities. In an exceptional combination of roles, Reb Hayyim Elazar Shapira was also the "Munkatcher Rebbe," head of a large hasidic following. A highly erudite scholar, he wrote a dozen volumes of responsa and other Torah works. In addition, he was an able administrator: he supervised the Darekhei Teshuvah *yeshiva in Munkatch, and headed a full-time* bet din, *consisting of five rabbis, which sat in daily session. Reb Hayyim Elazar was an extraordinarily charitable man who gave away most of his earnings. At his death, he left no material estate whatever.*

Sunday, Vayakhel-Pekudei, 5688 [1928]

It is written of Abraham our father, the first of our progenitors, "For I have known him, to the end that he may command his children and his household after him, that they may keep the way of the Lord, to do righteousness and justice . . ." and it is written that "no man knows his time. . . ." From my elders, I have learned [to do] like the great scholar, our revered teacher Rabbi Shlomo Kluger, of blessed memory, who wrote his first will when he was but fifty years of age. He wrote in support of it this allusion: "In this year of jubilee ye shall return every man unto his possession." Especially since I am, thank God, fifty-seven years old and I have passed a full jubilee plus another sabbatical year after the jubilee, I shall note down a number of things, with directions for good, in earnest entreaty and by full authority of the law of such testaments, that all of it be executed without any changes. With all this, I pray the Almighty, blessed be He, for length of days to fulfill His Torah and commandments and continue to benefit the public properly and, by light of day, await the coming of the Redeemer of Zion, speedily in our day, all of us together. And may I be preserved in life, together with the members of my family; may they have length of days in the midst of all Israel, Treasured People, let us merit salvation and redemption speedily.

₪ 1. First, I bow and bend the knee to the Almighty, blessed be He, Who formed and created me; and I confess all my many sins and transgressions, asking for forgiveness and a full repentant return. I hereby declare that the whole and sole intent in my innermost heart has been to serve Almighty God according to His will, to help bring about the perfection of the polity and hasten the coming of the Redeemer of Zion speedily and in our days, for this is the ultimate desire of the Almighty in creating the worlds—"last in creation, first in design"—that we merit redemption by virtue of our choices and life's tests, etc., as made known in the sacred books. And all intentions or words contrary to this are vanity, motivated by the Evil Inclination, and null and void in their very essence, as written in our prayerbooks in the Declaration [*moda'a*] following the *hatarat nedarim* on the eve of Rosh Hashanah about the practices of our holy sages and forefathers, may their merit protect us.

2. To all my household, including my daughter Frima and my students (whom I never called by this term in writing—and, as I explained in my essay, *Dibrei Torah*—not orally either; because they are to me like sons, like comrades, like *teachers*. "From my students I learned more than from anyone else" [*Ta'anit* 7a] as our talmudic sages state it. Considering all this, it is a mark of special affection for many when I refer to them as "my students," so I shall accede to their wishes this once, but even so, for the sake of expressing affection only), I pray you be careful to tread the path that is the path of our fathers, may their merit shield us, to adopt not the modern vogues, heaven forbid, but only reverence for God, all your lives; not to join any groups or organizations, including those who kick up their heels, the hypocrites and flatterers, like the *agudisten* [political Zionists] and the *yishuvisten* [those who settled in the Land of Israel or who believed in doing so], and their like. For their end is bitter, heaven protect us, and all contain heresy (God save us from their views), and postpone the redemption by reason of our sins, as we have already warned in concert with many of the great and saintly rabbis of this generation.

3. So also in matters of obscenity in dress and lewd uncovering of parts that should be covered: woe and alas, there is no obscenity or breach more serious than this, and these acts cause great harm to Israel and postponement of Jerusalem's reestablishment. Pray, then, take heed,

in particular our followers enumerated above, and my own offspring, may they attain to an old and good age, they, their sons, their daughters and wives. And my daughter Frima, may she achieve length of days and years, I caution strongly (and she will doubtless heed my words, God willing, to her benefit) with emphatic warning, to go about with kerchief on your head (begin doing so immediately after the twelve-month period) in the tradition of our ancestors, and as your mother does, may she flourish; and follow all seemly, modest ways. Even on weekdays, do not go, God forbid, with a "frisset," or with a "fall" resembling hair (because this is also forbidden according to the regulation cited in *Dibrei Hayyim* by our rabbi, may his merit protect us).

4. So, too, with the help of God, I trust that the remnant of Israel will do no injustice and on my [rabbinic] chair no outsider will sit, so that others will not inherit my honor, which is the honor of Torah, which is the honor of the Almighty, blessed be He and His faith. But rather that they will act in accordance with our tradition in general and in all details. This is my request and my behest in this matter; and may it be God's will that the source will not disappoint, the tree not be cut off but put forth worthy fruit.

5. Also, I emphatically caution my offspring, our followers, and our townspeople, may they all flourish, not to alter our sacred custom in matters pertaining either to public Torah study and the large, excellent group "Mahzikei Torah," or in all other religious matters like matzos for Pesach. So also the many other matters, and especially in my Bet Hamidrash, regarding the traditional ritual of our revered forefathers, may their merit shield us. So also our followers and comrades, wherever they are able to practice it, should establish the ritual of our fathers, together with the published prayer ritual. So also in all communal religious matters that I instituted, make efforts to maintain them with the extra fervor and strength of Torah.

Pertaining to burial arrangements:

Wrap me in the *tallis* which I was accustomed to wearing for the Sabbath afternoon service. It was my revered father's, may his merit preserve us; do not render any of the fringes unfit [as is customarily done].

Do not let my bier stay overly long; as written in the sacred *Zohar,* only as long as absolutely necessary. In all events, at the very longest only close to twenty-four hours from the time of expiration to the closing of the grave.

Do not eulogize me either over my bier or away from it. Especially do not say about me "righteous . . . pious . . . Torah genius . . ." for I am none of these. May the Almighty yet grant that I might return in true repentance, meditate on His Torah in fine detail, for length of days and years.

Earth of the Holy Land shall be placed on my knees, on my body, and some on my abdomen, but none on my face; only the customary pottery shards on my eyes.

I am as one who follows after giants; nonetheless, as was done for my revered father and master, place at the bottom of the grave under my body, on the ground, only a single board.

Let my bier be made out of the boards of my Shabbos table, just as our forefathers did, may their merit protect us.

Avrohom Mordekhai Alter (Gerer Rebbe)

Reb Avrohom Mordekhai Alter (1866 – 1945) was regarded as the outstanding member of the successful rabbinic dynasty of Gur. The Gur hasidim were a well-organized group under his effective leadership, despite the considerable dispersal of its members. Reb Avrohom journeyed to Eretz Yisrael several times before World War II. After the Nazis invaded Poland he found refuge in Warsaw. Then, in 1940, he managed to reach Eretz Yisrael.

With the help of God, Tevet 7, 5696 [Jan. 2, 1936]

I am seventy years old today, may the Almighty in His mercy lengthen my days and years, and I wish to write a testament in keeping with Scripture, "... that he may command his *children* ..." literally; and the latter part of that verse, "... and his household after him ..." referring to his associates and close friends, because Abraham dwelt, in his old age, in the house of study as stated in the Talmud (*Yoma* 28b). Therefore I too ask of you, my sons and my dear comrades, to observe the ways of God, blessed be He, to be just and upright and maintain peace among yourselves, be strong in the service of the Almighty, firm against all contemporary evils which are constantly with us, for there may well be new tests confronting us (as written in the *Zohar*) before the true redeemer comes. And if there be peace among you, then I too will fulfill my pledge to beseech the Almighty to bestow favor and kindness upon you.

The verse above [Gen. 18:19] makes a division between "his children" and "his household after him." His "household" are the associates and close friends—so you, take upon yourselves to observe the path of God justly and uprightly.

My beloved people of Israel, without any doubt I shall do all in my power to plead for favor and kindness on your behalf. I ask you to forgive me if I committed an injustice against anyone. In Midrash Tanhuma (at the end of Vaethanan) we learn how Moses our teacher asked the Children of Israel to forgive him for vexing them about the Torah and its commandments.

"Said Moses to Israel, 'Greatly have I grieved you . . . and now
me . . . as I forgive you.'"

From all the words of Moses we learn something, and fro
words we can learn not to cause our fellowmen anguish ev
matters of Torah and observances, but rather to do all in ways
and not pain. Further, we find in Midrash Tanhuma and in the
that Moses asked Israel to remember him and his remains; and
you, too, to remember me and my remains and say, "Woe unto.

Now, far be it from me, a thousand times over, as a low
unworthy being, to cite the words of Moses as applying to hims
not worthy of comparing myself to Moses our teacher, of
memory; however, in this instance I base myself in the dictur
sages, "The applications of Moshe Rabbenu's teachings apply i
generation and to every individual."

And now as the congregation needs a leader, I have delibera
decided to leave the leadership of our community in the hand
brother Reb Moshe Bezallel, may he flourish, my beloved com
whom I am bound heart, soul, and spirit. May he continue to dra
hearts near to our heavenly Father (as it is described by th
commentary in Tractate *Shabbat* 87a concerning Moses) and
draw mercy, blessing, and success from heaven in your behalf, a

Our sages taught [Tractate *Berakhot* 12a] that the entering wat
says to the outgoing watchman, "May He who caused His name to
in this house, cause love, friendships, peace, and fraternity to
among you." So I too wish you all these.

The Tosafists ask which benediction is it that may omit both the
Name and [mention of] His Kingdom. It seems to me that this is the
benediction resulting from unity within a Jewish community, for
itself is equivalent to the Divine Name and Kingdom. As they
further, "Greeting one's fellow by name and where unity exists, th
also present God's name." Similarly, "Kingdom" is also present, a
ing to Rashi—namely, full blessing prevails by virtue of "the gather
the leaders of the people—when they gather together in one ban
peace reigns among them, *that* is God's Kingdom, but not when
divides them."

God's mercies to one so unworthy as myself have enabled me to live to see descendants numbering close to one hundred souls; I plead with all of you to observe God's ways and to act justly. May it be His will that all of you will serve the Almighty, blessed be He. I ask that all of you act in accord with the precepts of Judaism, and with respect to marriages, that each match be only with the daughter of a *talmid hakham* [scholar].

Now I caution strongly against publishing all my writings; rather, destroy the majority of them and only the smaller portion, found suitable by the critical evaluation of my brothers and brother-in-law, shall remain. For there are things I wrote in my youth that need to be destroyed.

A stringent warning: Burn what is found to be unsuitable, as I instructed my son Reb Bunim, may he flourish.

If there is anyone who wishes to go to a different rebbe, let him do as his heart desires and let no one quarrel with him, Heaven forbid.

Yehuda Leib Graubart (The Stashever Rav)

Rabbi Yehuda Leib Graubart, chief rabbi of Toronto, Canada, from 1922 to 1936, was renowned both in Europe and America as a great halakhic scholar and author. An eloquent orator and an influential leader of Mizrahi, he was a strong proponent of Eretz Yisrael in the decades before Zionism was widely accepted among Orthodox Jews. Note the concern Rabbi Graubart expresses about the return of borrowed books. In general, remaining a debtor, in money or any tangibles, at death is a serious concern for the ethically scrupulous; books are a special concern too, because in Jewish tradition one may not refuse to lend a book.

Regarding the will which I wrote on the 14th of Menahem-Ab 5694 [July 26, 1934], and the several details added to it on Nisan 19, 5696 [April 11, 1936]: Both are written in the language of the land [English], devised in accordance with the law in the most effective manner, and let no heir contest it.

Please return the borrowed books in my possession: the volumes belonging to the Etz Hayyim school. Also, return these volumes to the Bet Hamidrash in Stashov (*Magen Avraham* published in Johannesburg, *Hoq Ya'akov, Ikkarei Arba'ah Turim*); to Notte Meir of Stashov (*Sidre Teharah*), to the rabbi there, Rabbi Yitzhak Meir (*Sha'ar Mishpat*, two volumes *Shoshanat Ya'akov*); to Asher Nussbaum there (*Sefer Derush Ashre Hatzevi*).

I caution you in strongest terms not to eulogize me (except if my sons are here). [Place] my grave only beside a poor, honest man who earned his living by the work of his hands. The gravestone should be of utmost simplicity; inscribe no titles, only my name, the name of my sainted father, of blessed memory, and the family name.

On the eve of Nisan 20, 5696 [April 12, 1936]
(The year and the Sidre Tzav)
Distribute charity on that day [of burial]

Part Two

WILLS FROM
THE HOLOCAUST

The Holocaust poured out on the world a measure of malevolence and bestiality unprecedented in human history. Its martyred victims, like their more fortunate brethren elsewhere, wished to leave an expression of their in-most thoughts to survivors and coming generations. Even the pitiably few surviving wills and letters reveal a wide range of individual response to the unbelievable catastrophe which overtook their writers. Some demand vengeance and a continuing fight to the death with the cruel oppressor and all that he represents. Others, to our everlasting wonder, reveal a struggle to maintain the author's divine image and human dignity in the face of incomparable evil.

Hirsch Moshe Zaddok

This will was written by the last Jew of Kovno, Hirsch Moshe Zaddok. It was written inside the cover of a book, and was discovered by the writer's brother, who escaped Kovno at the start of the war and returned with the victorious Soviet forces.

To every man and woman! They treated us like animals in the forest. Seven days and nights we hid in an attic with no food or water. The heat was fierce. On the eighth day they rained grenades on us and torched the building. We managed to reach the cellar but the entire building was engulfed in flames over our heads.

Brothers! Avenge us! We were once more than fifty thousand souls in Kovno and now there remain but a few. We too await the end. Our revenge will come when you destroy the very last of the wild beasts!

Show them no mercy, just as they had no pity on us. Repay them for all their crimes on behalf of all those they tortured and killed. Only then will mankind be rid of these snakes who dare call themselves humans. Brothers! *Vengeance*—this must be your sacred mission in life.

Hirsch Moshe Zaddok
One of the Jewish victims

A Mother's Will

Published in the ghetto newspaper Warsaw-Krakow, 1940, this will was signed only "Your Mother."

Judaism, my child, is the struggle to bring down God upon earth, a struggle for the sanctification of the human heart. This struggle your people wages not with physical force but with spirit, with sincere, heartfelt prayers, and by constant striving for truth and justice.

So do you understand, my child, how we are distinct from others and wherein lies the secret of our existence on earth?

Knowing this, will your heart still be heavy, my child? Will you still say you cannot stand your fate? But you must, my child, for so were you commanded; it is your calling. This is your mission, your purpose on earth.

You must go to work alongside people of other nations . . . and you will teach them that they must come to a brotherhood of nations and to a union of all nations with God.

You may ask, "How does one speak to them?" This is how: "Thou shalt not murder; thou shalt not steal; thou shalt not covet; love thy neighbor as thyself. . . ." Do these things and through their merit, my child, you will be victorious.

Zippora Birman

The writer, a member of the Jewish fighting group in the Bialystok ghetto, fell in the defense of the ghetto in August 1943. Her notes were discovered after the war.

All is lost. This is our fate, to atone for the sins of the preceding generations.

We mourned all of them, we grieved over their loss; the most horrible possibility in history has happened to us. We witnessed, we heard, we anguished; and now we have been sentenced to be silenced forever. Our bones will not even be brought to decent Jewish burial. Unbearable. There is no choice but to die with honor, along with the thousands who go to their deaths without fear, without fright. We *know*: the Jewish people will not disappear. It will return to life, grow and bloom again, and will avenge our blood that is spilled.

So I address you, comrades, wherever you may be: You have the obligation to avenge. Day and night, take no rest from this charge— avenge the blood that is spilled—just as we have no respite here, face-to-face with death.

Cursed is he who reads this, mournfully sighs, and returns to his daily tasks.

It is not mourning that we demand of you! We did not even mourn our own parents, but speechless and silent we viewed the heaped corpses of our loved ones who were shot like dogs.

We call upon you: Vengeance, vengeance—with no mercy, with no sentimentality, with no "good" Germans. For the "good" German let it be an easier death; let him be killed last. That is what they promised the Jews of whom they approved: "You will be shot last."

This is our demand, the demand of all of us. This is the burning appeal of human beings who likely will be among the fallen, who will fight with courage and die with dignity.

To vengeance do we call you, you who were not imprisoned in Hitler's hell; this is our summons, and you are compelled to fulfill it, even at the risk of death.

Our crushed bones, scattered to all corners of Europe, will know no repose and the ashes of our corpses, scattered to the winds, will have no rest until you avenge us.

Remember this and do it. It is our plea—it is your duty.

Among the Embers: Martyrs' Testaments

These five wills, brief and hurriedly written, speak for themselves. All five appeared in Mime Hashoah Vehagevura, *published by Yad Vashem in Jerusalem.*

Written by the last twelve Jews to be murdered at the death camp at Chelmno, in January 1945. Before their deaths, they defended themselves and killed a number of Germans.

If any relatives or friends of these individuals are left alive, then be informed that all the Jews who were removed from Lodz were killed most brutally; they were tortured, then burned in fire. Be well. If you survive, avenge our blood.

Carved on the wall of the synagogue in Kovel, signed by David Elster, Sept. 15, 1942.

A chill passes through us . . . here come our murderers, dressed up . . . their filthy hands adorned in white gloves, they herd us two-by-two . . . tender-hearted brothers and sisters . . . O how hard it is to part from this beautiful world forever . . . let no one who remains alive ever forget— Jewish boys and girls from our Jewish street, innocent of any wrong-doing. Wreak vengeance on our murderers.

The will of the members of "Dror": signed by Sheindel Schwartz, Leah Fish, Rachel Fogelman, and David Aisenberg. These words were written on the wall of the Kovel synagogue in which the Jews were concentrated before being taken to be killed.

Greetings to our comrades from a group of *halutzim* about to die. We remained faithful to our cause to the end. Avenge our blood that is spilled.

Part of a will written by a woman of Kovel, to her husband; carved on the synagogue wall.

Reuben Atlas, this is to inform you that here, in this place, your wife Gina and your son Imosz were murdered. Our child cried bitterly; he did not want to die. Go forth to battle and avenge the blood of your wife and your only son. We die for no crime whatever.

Gina Atlas

The will of a young woman, written on the same synagogue wall.

I am a daughter of Israel, twenty years old. O how lovely is the world about us! Why should they destroy us when everything within me desires and yearns for life. Have my last minutes really arrived? Vengeance! Come and avenge me, whoever reads this last request of mine.

These lines, written in chalk on a small board, were found by one of the Jews brought in by the Nazis to clear the streets of the Warsaw Ghetto after the Uprising. The charred board was found next to the bodies of a Jewish couple.

Fellow Jews, when you find us, bury my dear wife and me according to our Jewish faith. I request that you say Kaddish three times—for my little eight-year-old son, for my devoted wife, and for me. We lived, we loved each other, we fought, and believed in the God of Israel.

Berl Tomshelski

This note was written to the Blozhever Rebbe by a Polish Jew just before going to his death. The recipient survived the war and read it at a meeting in New York, reported in the Morgen Journal, *Jan. 14, 1946.*

Dear Rebbe:

I write you these lines a few minutes before I go to sanctify God's name. Soon they come to take me to the ovens. I beg you, dear rebbe, if

God saves you from this, then for heaven's sake, perpetuate my name and my wife's name. If you are in Eretz Yisrael, please drive a stone into the holy ground in our names; and if you come to America, please write a Torah scroll in our memory.

The Chief Rabbi of Grodzisk

Since ancient times Jewish sources have described the period leading to the coming of the messiah as characterized by "birth pangs." The travail of childbirth was seen as analogous to the tribulations and agonies which would precede the birth of the new era. The rabbi of Grodzisk referred to this oft-expressed belief in his exhortation to several thousand of his fellow Jews as he and they were led to the gas chambers. The event was reported to the late Chief Rabbi Isaac Herzog during his tour of Displaced Persons camps in Italy.

Brothers and sisters! One of our sages in talmudic times said in his days: "Let him come, but let me not see him" [*Sanhedrin* 98b]. That is to say, let the Messiah come, so long as I don't have to see him. That sage did not want to witness the great agonies with which Israel would be afflicted preceding the coming of the redeemer. However, he may have allowed himself to make such a request because in his days the time of redemption was still very distant. But now, at the hour when we stand on the threshhold of the redemption proper, now as we wash and purify with our blood the path of the redeemer, at the time we purify with our ashes, like the ashes of the Red Heifer, the people of Israel, to render it worthy of greeting the Messiah of righteousness, now we are forbidden to speak thus. On the contrary, we are obliged to see ourselves as fortunate that it fell to our lot to blaze a path for the redeemer and to accept with love our binding upon the alter of the sanctification of God's revered name. Come, then, my fellow Jews, and let us recite joyfully "Shema Yisrael."

With song on their lips they approached and entered the gas chambers.

On the Walls of Bialystok Prison

On the walls of Cell 81 in the infamous Bialystok prison one sees many names inscribed and a number of still-decipherable messages in familiar Yiddish script. Here many Jews spent their last hours before death. These are the surviving traces of their tragic fate.

Berkowicz, Grodno, was killed here, July 15, 1944, seven o'clock in the morning. Convey greetings in Moscow to Kilgin Samuel Georgevitch.

Isaac Kulbin was killed here July 15, 1944, for the Jewish people. Take revenge!

Born in Bielsk-Podliaski in 1921. The whole family was killed in the prison. The last Jew—Henekh Hoffman. I go to my death with head high. I greet my comrades, the brothers Okon and Posnanskin. Avenge me. They tortured me. I betrayed no one. Avenge us.

Avenge us! This is written by Berl Hirshenboim of Grodno. Twenty Jews from Bialystok and Grodno are spending their last night here. We are living through our last minutes. We await our death. Today is one month. 15/7/44

Berl Schatzman. I sit manacled in chains and await death. August 1944.

The following letter was received by the Blozhever Rebbe, who survived the war. It was written on a Sabbath eve, in winter 1942.

My dear rabbi, Reb Israel Shapiro, may you flourish:

They have surrounded the Burstin Factory in which 800 Jews work, and they are going to annihilate us. They are still undecided whether to shoot us here in Lemberg or take us to Bergen-Belsen to gas us. ... I must hurry because the order has already come to strip. They're going to shoot us here.

My sister's children are with the Christian, Voshilevski, in Greiding [Latvia]. So I ask you to devote your efforts to take them from there and deliver them into Jewish hands. Whatever happens happens, but let them remain Jews. My wife, Shevah bat Hannah, they shot yesterday.

I hope that after my death I will be able to approach your holy ancestors and convey greetings from you and to intercede on your behalf for long life.

Your servant,
Arieh ben Leah Korn

Shulamit Rabinovitch

These letters were written by Shulamit Rabinovitch and her husband from the Kovno Ghetto. They were grandchildren of Rabbi Yitzhak Elchanan Spektor and devoted communal workers in Kovno before and during the war. The letters were addressed to their sons in the United States. We stand in awe of the ethical sensitivity of this couple: The wife takes pride in the fact that her husband did not take advantage of his position to show favoritism to the members of his own family. We also note the date as D-Day.

June 6, 1944

My dear, fortunate sons!

We sense the end is near. It will not be long before they finish us off. On one hand it is good, on the other hand very bad, to die right now. Good that we have lived to see the end come; and bad to die now, a moment before the redemption.

Actually it is not difficult for me to die, or for Papa either. What is very hard, infinitely hard, is the fact that your young brother Shmuel will die when we do. And he is such a wonderful boy. Even under the most brutal conditions he developed into a fine human being; perhaps with less formal education, but with so much humane feeling and refinement, that it would be truly worthwhile for him to remain alive. How few of those who suffered this treatment retained the human image! The struggle for existence is hard and everyone wants to live, to save himself; the law of the jungle is dominant: "Save yourself if you can."

But you may be very proud of your father. He is among those who never took advantage of his public office, never put Shmuel or me ahead of the other sufferers for whom he was responsible. How we wish you could have some knowledge about these past three painful years. I hope that some will survive and that you will receive some word about our sufferings and our dying. It is now in its fourth year and the end is approaching. It didn't really pay for us to hold out and suffer so long and then not to survive. Were *they* the righteous ones (if there is such a thing), those who were first to go? For years we learned so much, suffered so much. We could teach others so very much, and it is too bad that it all comes to nothing, along with us. Were we to be rescued, we could dry up the oceans, and demonstrate with how little a person can get along! If I could only bequeath you the ability to get along with little and the ability to do everything for yourself, then you, being free, could never be unhappy.

I have already written you several letters with various dates and have left them for you at a number of locations. I doubt, however, whether you will receive them.

Our greatest consolation and good fortune is that you are not here. But, dear children, don't take foolish things to heart. Be happy, contented people; be good human beings and loyal sons of your oppressed nation. Never abandon your land or your people. Fight for freedom and social justice. Be just and honest; and under normal conditions this is so easy! We speak of you very often, and you are our consolation. Whenever Muka gets very depressed, he says: "Mama, how I'd like to see Amos and Nioma again."

There is still a remnant left here of your friends, boys as well as girls. They mention you often with affection and with ungrudging envy. Know how to appreciate your good fortune and use it not for yourselves alone but for others both near and distant. Lighten the life of your grandfather, grandmother, aunts, and uncles who have also survived. And don't mourn for us with tears and words, but rather with deeds. We were not useless here; in any way we could we tried to make things easier for those around us. I am leaving the world with almost a clear conscience. I lived my life. I have no complaints to anyone. It is a matter of fate; I believe in *beshert,* that things are destined. But why Muka? That is our greatest sorrow. I regret that I cannot communicate to you everything we have experienced. You will probably know something; but whatever you will ever hear and know, the reality is a thousand times more horrible and more painful. Words don't exist to tell it; no colors exist with which to represent it.

I hope you are under the influence of your grandfather, grandmother, and Aunt Jennie. Obey them and be good people. Too young you have become orphans. But better to be orphans there than to be with father and mother here. I kiss you very warmly. Kiss and greet all those near to me, whoever may be there. After all, I know nothing about anyone, just as no one knows about us. We have been buried alive here for three years now.

Your mother

Shulamit Rabinovitch's Husband

This letter, also dated June 6, 1944, was written by the husband of Shulamit Rabinovitch, and accompanied her letter to their children in the United States.

June 6, 1944

Dear and beloved sons:

I reproved your mother, telling her that her letter to you was transformed into a will. I don't know at all how much longer we are destined to be tormented; our fate lies in wait for us. But even a life of suffering is life, and we constantly wonder at how much a human being can bear.

Perhaps these lines will come into your hands by some unbelievable chance. If so, we want you to know that during the summer of 1944 your parents were still alive, thinking often of you, and completely devoid of hope of ever receiving any message from you.

Materially speaking this past year has not been the worst. Also, in my position I have seen and have been saturated by so much anguish and have borne so much sorrow that one becomes hardened, and one wonders how it was possible to live through it all.

Even more, one is in awe over the will-to-live and the power of resistance of the surviving remnant present here.

Meanwhile we have beautiful summer days. Through the window we can see the greening of the little garden, tended by Youngest Son. The roads are sandy here; who knows whether we will end our days here or be forced to relocate farther still.

Be well and strong.

The God of Abraham, Isaac, and Jacob shield and protect you.

WILLS FROM THE LAND OF ISRAEL

The Land of Israel is multifaceted; it presents us its many faces, evolved out of its unique history and as the result of its special relationship to the People of Israel.

Over the centuries and to the present moment its people have come to it for many reasons and have responded to it variously. Some came to be buried in the holy ground on which walked the patriarchs and prophets; many came to build the Land, to live on it and to be up-built by it; some built philanthropic bridges to it from afar, then came to forge personal links with it; many came to pioneer and to build a just society based on Jewish values; and many have been there always, manning the barricades of Torah, seen as the first line of defense for the Holy Land and its People. Many came in this century to live in peace, but were impelled to fight in defense of the Land and the People of Israel, some to die for it, in distant lands.

The ethical wills in this section reflect the diversity of meaning Israel the Land has had for the Jews and how they have responded to its influence and its call.

Menahem Mendel of Vitebsk

Reb Menahem Mendel of Vitebsk arrived in Safed in 1777 to live out his years in the Holy Land and to be buried in its sacred soil. This has been a common desire over the centuries and is almost the sole concern of his will. A disciple of the hasidic master, the Maggid of Mezeritch, Reb Menahem Mendel led a contingent of Hasidim and non-Hasidim from Eastern Europe who wished to settle in Safed, a focus and center for the mystically motivated. He died in 1788.

With the help of God, in the sacred city of Safed, may it be speedily rebuilt, Amen, Elul 5, 5537 [1777], the date of my safe arrival from abroad to the Holy Land, may it be speedily rebuilt in our day, Amen.

I have decided to list several things to be done after the close of my span of days and years in our Holy Land. It is my plan and my desire to live here in this holy city, may it be rebuilt, as it is written, ". . . he shall live by them." * But if, heaven forbid, it is decreed (despite the teachings of the sages that the atmosphere of the Land of Israel makes one wise) that I should be of unsound mind at that time, I therefore now write down these nine items:

1. I request of the Sacred Brotherhood that precisely within an hour after my soul has departed, my body no longer be in this world.

2. They shall dress me specifically in the garments I brought with me from abroad.

3. They are not to place me in a coffin.

4. Those who carry the bier are not to speak at all, even on matters of Torah. Let them rather meditate on true repentance; I shall be at that time in a state to which even the perfectly righteous cannot attain, hence no evil spirit or harm can have influence, heaven forbid.

5. At the cemetery, do not put me down on the ground with the bier as customary, but rather carry me on the bier to the gravesite and from the bier [place me] directly into the grave—without boards, but directly on the sacred soil.

6. At the moment of covering my eyes with pottery shard as customary

*Lev. 18:5. The intent here is that since settling in the Holy Land is an observance of great merit, its observance earns one length of days.

... pronounce the name of the sainted Ba'al Shem Tov, of blessed memory, and the name of my sainted master the Maggid of Mezeritch, of blessed memory.

7. Let the participants afterward immerse in a kosher *mikvah,* specifically in the kind called *perisha.**

8. They are not to do any "circuits" because this will extend the time beyond the hour mentioned above in paragraph 1.

9. All my clothes, both of Sabbath and holy days and of weekdays, including my overcoat with the silver buttons, shall be distributed among the *poor,* explicitly.

Now I will pray to God, blessed be He, to lengthen my days and years in goodness and in pleasantness.

---

*The reference here is to a *mikvah,* ritual pool, incorporating specifications even more exacting than the stringent requirements for the design of the ordinary *mikvah.*

Elijah David Rabinovitz (Teomim)

Rabbi Elijah David Rabinovitz (1843 – 1905) was appointed as the first Ash-
kenazic chief rabbi of Jerusalem in 1900, a post he filled brilliantly but briefly,
until 1905. Among the changes he wrought was the institution of a system of
official inspection services for supervising the weights and measures used by
local merchants. We note in his tzava'ah *the intense introspection and the*
preoccupation with improvement of personal traits which are both typical of
the true ba'al musar *(moralist), and his scrupulous care in the performance of*
the mezuzah *and tefillin observances.*

All my lilfe I have despised conceit. From earliest childhood I have felt
revulsion for a person in whom I detected signs of arrogant pride. It
seems to me that there is in my heart not the least bit of arrogance.
Although I often see clearly what my few skills and positive attributes
are, I thank God that I am not moved to pride over them.

Love of money never found a place in my heart. Still, I cannot claim
purity of heart to the extent of *despising* money; I have not yet attained to
that trait. But to love money—no.

So also have I always disliked personal glory, and I always feel
wretched when people honor me. Especially is this so when I am given
honor by those greater and better than I . . . always have I received more
honor than I deserve. Nor can I dissuade people from doing this since,
as set forth in the Talmud [Jerusalem Talmud Tractate *Sheviit,* end],
doing so causes them to attribute the trait of *modesty* to me as well! So
what am I to do? These precious traits are an inheritance from my
revered father and teacher, of blessed memory.

So also has truth been a lamp unto my feet, and I have hated falsehood, despising it exceedingly. I never covered up the faults of loved
ones or of my relatives whenever it was contrary to the truth, nor will I
take liberties with the truth, even inwardly perverting strict truth; nor
make excuses improperly when something turns out wrong, denying
responsibility for an outcome. These latent characteristics are also
bequeathed me by my father, of blessed memory. And though the term
"modest" was fitting and proper for *him*, in whom the trait of modesty

was truly present, since he had much of which to be proud, not so is the case with me, who am but "dregs of the wine . . ." [Jerusalem Talmud Tractate *Ma'asrot* III, 50d] for of what value am I and my deeds. I recognize in my little worth and very limited knowledge that I have nothing whatever to boast of, so the trait of modesty does not apply at all; simply and literally stated, I am and possess nothing. But this I can say with certainty: that source of all evil, that foremost of impure traits— *arrogance*—is something I have despised to the ultimate degree, even the slightest hint of it. It is the root of all transgressions, the major ones and the minor ones alike, among human beings. Whoever has the slightest trace of it cannot remain free of guilt. I thank God that it has not found a place in my heart until now; may the Almighty protect me from it for the remainder of my life.

Love for the sacred Torah and for those who study it, especially for the greatest of these scholars and for the truly God-fearing, is rooted in my heart and soul. To this day I yearn to stand and minister to those great, thoroughly pious geniuses, simply to serve them as a servant ministers to his master. To my regret I have not yet been privileged to do this. Where I am known this is denied me, and elsewhere the opportunity has not been present. I always keep before my mind's eye the sayings of our holy sages, "Let your fellow's honor be as dear to you as your own" [*Avot*. 2:15], and "whoever recognizes that his fellow excels him even in one thing is obliged to pay him homage" [*Avot* 6:3]. I am therefore careful in treating others with respect, especially anyone who is my superior in something, for the sages have imposed an obligation upon us to honor such individuals.

Because of my habit to avoid honors, I have been retiring and socially withdrawn. I have not shown my writings and religious compositions to any but a very small number of my closest friends. This was in order to avoid experiencing conceit from seeing many writings in print. On the front page of every one of my compositions I have written the aphorism of Rabbi Yohanan ben Zakkai, "If you have learned much Torah, do not credit yourself for it" [*Avot* II, 9].

I have always exercised care in honoring those greater and older than

I, in not writing to them "Dear friend," as if imposing myself upon them by virtue of the correspondence.

From my earliest days I have been careful to set aside a tithe of all profits that came my way. In the observance of timely recitation of the *Shema* I have been scrupulous since my earliest youth; and it is now about twenty years since I have become accustomed to recite the *Shema* just before sunrise, in fulfillment of the view of a number of ancient sages who specify that the morning recitation of the *Shema* is before sunrise.

Regarding public worship, I have been very careful, with God's help. Sometimes it necessitated great effort to assemble ten for a quorum, and to this day when I must pray alone I feel as if I haven't prayed at all!

For the past several decades I have trained myself to wear small tefillin all day, especially when, en route, I am away from my studies. In such cases I take comfort in the words of the sage in the *Mekhilta*, "Donning the tefillin is considered equivalent to studying Torah." For the past several years I have developed the habit of wearing several different pair of tefillin every day, because of the risk that a single pair may be ritually imperfect; with several pair this risk is eliminated.

All my life I have never been slow to perform deeds of personal service to others; my hands are not tied to prevent my gathering alms for the poor, and my feet are not chained to prevent my going from door to door for charitable donations.

Many are the sufferings and travails that have overtaken me, may you be spared such troubles, and these have aged me before my time. But nothing brings me to tears so quickly as when I remember Jerusalem, our holy city and house of glory, the exile of God's Presence, the exile of Torah and of Israel, the memories of which cause my eyes to flood with tears.

Before I undertook rabbinical duties all my thoughts were tied to matters of Torah. Even in conversation with people my mind was on Torah. It has been a favorite saying of mine that this is the literal meaning of the verse "Thou shalt meditate on it day and night" [Josh. 1:8].

For many years now I follow the practice of observing the commandment of *mezuzah* in every detail. Thus whenever I rent a new flat (in which *mezuzah* observance is not by biblical but by rabbinic injunction, according to most authorities) I purchase one room from the owner, for cash, for a specified period in a way that it belongs to me fully by Torah law. In this way I am able to afix the *mezuzah* immediately, while a renter is obligated only after thirty days. One thing is certain: dwelling in one's own house obligates a *mezuzah* from the first hour, according to the Torah.

With anything owned by another I always exercise great care; and I avoided coveting another's possession. I have been guided by the interpretation of the *Eben Ha'ezer* on this negative commandment, namely, that the property of another is simply unattainable under any circumstances, and is repugnant to me like the flesh of pig and other forbidden things.

Whenever I preached in public, on the Sabbath before Passover and on the Sabbath of Return, I always announced beforehand, "I am prepared to observe the commandment 'Thou shalt surely rebuke thy neighbor. . . .' [Lev. 19:17]. May it be God's will that my words be well ordered and well received in the service of the Almighty, and that I not miss the mark by offending anyone, God forbid." With God's help I have always been careful in this regard in every possible way. May He also preserve me in the days ahead for good.

Naftali Amsterdam

One of the disciples of Rabbi Israel of Salant, founder of the Musar movement, Rabbi Naftali Amsterdam (1832 – 1916) was himself one of its pillars. He was rabbi in Helsinki, Finland, from 1867 to 1875, then served in a number of Eastern European communities before settling in Jerusalem in 1906. He helped establish the Musar movement there. These selections from his will reflect the lifelong preoccupation of the true ba'al musar *with ethical self-improvement.*

First, I request of you firmly that after my death no eulogy shall be made for me; neither in Kovno nor here in Jerusalem shall any eulogy be delivered over me.

In general I can tell you this: what truly set me on my feet regarding God's service was only *musar* study, after the manner of my revered teacher and master, of blessed memory, who used to repeat the rabbinic adage "Whoever departs from the Torah is consumed by fire . . ." [Tractate *Baba Batra* 79a] numerous times, aloud, with lips afire and with great fervor. On any day in which I study *musar*, I find my actions, my words and thoughts, to be of better quality. The manner and order of this activity is as I learned them from my master and teacher [Rabbi Israel Salant]: One should divide his study of *musar* into two parts. For example, if one can devote one hour to this pursuit, let him divide the hour into two parts. Devote a half hour for studying a *musar* book in the customary, sequential manner of other studies, giving heed to the ideas of sources like *Mesillat Yesharim* [*The Ways of the Just*] or *Hovot Halevavot* [*Duties of the Heart*] and the like. The second half hour should be for studying a given segment in penetrating depth, reviewing it many times, again and again, be it *Hovot Halevavot* or *Reshit Hokhmah* [*Beginning of Wisdom*], a saying from *Pirke Avot* [*Ethics of the Fathers*], or similar source. This was his regimen of study.

Foremost is the need for an individual to improve his traits of character. For this, two things are essential: first, the study of *musar*; second, a good comrade is necessary. At specified times they should study together the subject of improving one's ethical traits and seek ways of achieving this. A good way of doing this is with a partner, devoting each day of the week to a different trait. For example, on Sunday one can work on correcting the trait of anger, on Monday, impatience, and so on, developing the habits of careful speech, caring for others. (The latter trait is extremely important because it encompasses and improves many negative traits. I once asked my revered master to suggest a way to cure the habit of a bad temper; he replied that one should perform deeds of personal kindness for others, and the bad temper would correct itself.) Even better, you can divide the month into weeks and devote an entire week to each trait.

Concerning prayer: One should avoid letting obtrusive thoughts enter his mind during the *Amidah*. Admittedly this is one of the most difficult things to avoid, because without willing it disordered thoughts come tumbling in. Still, I have devised a partial solution to this problem, and that is to concentrate on the rabbinic reasons for the specific sequence of the benedictions, as detailed in Tractate *Megillah*. Doing this helps one focus on the meanings of the words in the prayers thus excluding external thoughts. Another suggestion is to pause a bit every so often and maintain silence. I myself have always paused at three points in the *Amidah*—at *attah honen, teka beshofar,* and *retze.* During this silent pause it is good to keep in mind before Whom you stand: before the King of Kings, the Holy One, praised be He.

Theodor Herzl

Theodor Herzl (1860 – 1904), founder of the World Zionist Organization and acclaimed father of modern political Zionism, was born in Budapest. His background was in the spirit of the German-Jewish Enlightenment. Herzl earned a doctorate in law and worked for a time in the courts in Vienna before embarking on a writing career in 1885. During the next few years he published half a dozen books and many plays, most of which were staged in Germany and Austria to public acclaim. Contrary to popular belief, Herzl was aware of and involved in the Jewish question long before the Dreyfuss Affair. His drama Das Neue Ghetto *was written and presented in order to stimulate public discussion of the problem of anti-Semitism. It was the attitude of the French public during the Dreyfuss trial, which Herzl covered for the Vienna* Freie Presse, *that brought him to a crystallization of his ideas about a territory of their own for Jews. Herzl sacrificed years of his life as well as a successful writing career for the Zionist ideal.*

It is fitting to prepare for the day of death. One cannot speak in flowery language.

What I have meant for Jews, future days will tell better than the general public in my own time. My primary estate consists of diary entries about my activities in Jewish affairs. They comprise, to date, four books, a portion of which are being kept at father's and the remainder with me. I shall perhaps place them in a more secure place. These memoirs shall be published immediately following my death.

For the purpose of publishing them, for the style editing, etc., a committee shall be appointed.

To this committee, the Austrian Zionist Federation shall appoint two members; the guardian of my children shall appoint a literary adviser who shall be, if possible, from among my circle of friends.

A contract is to be signed with a proper publishing house for the publication of the writings in German and English. The contractual-legal aspects entailed in this rests upon the guardian of my children.

It will be desirable, perhaps, to publish as well a collection of my Zionist articles and addresses.

The conditions for this shall be the same as for the publication of my memoirs.

Similarly, I suggest seeking a publisher for the rest of my writings.

I believe that all my plays should be published in one volume.

My favorite play is *The Ghetto*. Also, the fragment *Marriage Comedy* which I began writing in Wiesbaden shall be included in the collection; furthermore, incorporate the notes to serve as a curiosity for creative artists. One volume shall contain the feuilletons and the articles which I wrote from Paris to the *Neue Freie Presse* and which have never been assembled in a book.

The rest of my feuilletons, which have not yet been gathered into a book, will fill several volumes.

My name will grow after my death; I therefore believe that a publisher will be found for all my writings.

I know today, as I have known every single minute since I began my writing career, that I wielded my pen as an honest man.

Never did I sell my pen, never did I utilize it for base or obscene purposes, not even for social reasons.

It is permitted to publish this last testament.

Even after my death no one will gainsay my words.

Officially recorded in the district court of the state, at Wahring, July 4, 1904.

Edmond James de Rothschild

A scion of the famous banking family in France, Edmond de Rothschild (1845 – 1934) became involved in active support of the Yishuv, *the Jewish community in Palestine, during the Russian pogroms of the 1880s. Because of his strong desire for anonymity, he was, in the early days, referred to as "Hanadiv Hayadu'a," the "Well-Known Benefactor." His support took many forms: he gave direct support to developing colonies, underwrote long-term agricultural experiments by experts sent from France, and purchased large tracts of land later transferred to the ownership of the Jewish authorities in Palestine. The settlement of Binyamina was named in his honor. The following is from a statement of his credo delivered at the Great Synagogue in Tel Aviv on May 17, 1925, on his final visit to Palestine. The framed text is hung on the east wall of the synagogue.*

To the Rock of Israel I lift up my heart and thank Him with all my soul for His kindness to me, for the privilege of beholding at my advanced age this wondrous sight, the vision of Israel restored. When I call to memory the past, about fifty years ago when I first began my work, when I recall the appearance of the land, strewn with stones, full of thorn and thistle, its inhabitants struggling to produce meager kernels from the poor soil, it is as though I were in a dream. It never occurred to me that *all* Jews would be gathered in Eretz Yisrael; today, too, this remains an impossibility. What was in my heart was the establishment of a center, one that is as significant as possible, for the enhancement of the spirit of Judaism and its exalted Torah and its noble culture; and that this center would exert a beneficial influence upon the condition of Jews in all the countries of the world.

They used to say to me, "You are building on sand!" Now, here is the sand and, in the words of the psalmist, it has become a cornerstone* in the rebuilding of Israel. The fields are cultivated, the numerous vineyards and orchards are like oases in the desert—all giving testimony to the energy and endurance of the Jewish people.

The fact that the great powers accepted the [Balfour] Declaration, and

*An allusion to Rosh Pina, one of the earliest settlements which Rothschild maintained, and to the verse, "The stone which the builder rejected is become the chief cornerstone [*rosh pina*]" in Psalms 118:22.

that the League of Nations approved it as well, seems like the realization of the prophecy which sustained the spirit of our ancestors throughout the many centuries of anguish and travail. Now, after two thousand years, the utterances of the prophets are being fulfilled before our eyes: "Surely the isles shall wait for me, the ships of Tarshish first, to bring thy sons from afar" [Isa. 60:9]. Happy are we to live in a blessed time as this when we may add, "Certainly, this is the day that we have looked for; we have found, we have seen it" [Lam. 2:16].

Long ago, when I visited the settlements for the first time, I was impressed by the Hebrew studies in the schools. After several years I was happy to observe that Hebrew had become a living tongue. Jews who came from various lands could communicate in one language; and this language served also as a link between the past and present and also as a bond with the ideals of the forefathers.

Basing myself on what I have done in Eretz Yisrael, I wish to tell how, in my opinion, the National Home ought to develop so that it not founder on shoals born of false hopes, and how to clear away the stumbling-blocks which may cause you to trip if you stray from the course.

First, you must be concerned about intensifying and enlarging the ideal of the National Home in every possible way and to work with all your might for its fruition. Its blossoming will help all the inhabitants of the land. You must continue to live, as heretofore, in the best relations with your neighbors and thereby be true to the principles transmitted to us by our ancestors: "Love thy neighbor as thyself" [Lev. 19:18].

The Jewish people in their land cannot exist by virtue of physical energies alone, without a connection to our noble past and to our tradition. What can a small group of Jews in a tiny corner of the world do against the storms that uproot even the mighty powers of the world. You cannot survive even a small gale; you would be like a wind-blown straw, like a fleeting cloud.

In all that you try to do—both in your daily work and in your exalted tasks—you must follow the ideals of Judaism, act in accord with its clear guidelines, toward that moral perfection that is the essence of our faith. An eternal Law of the highest spirituality, this is the Law the Israelites received two thousand years ago at a time when all surrounding peoples were barbaric, steeped in their abominable practices. These are the ideals that preserved the Jewish people, living and enduring, maintained its strength and courage these thousands of years.

The Tablets of the Covenant which Moses received at Mount Sinai, and whose remembrance we celebrate a few days hence on the festival of Shavuot, have remained to this day the basis of all civilization. While Israelites wandered in the desert, the Ark of the Covenant went before them constantly, and in it were the tablets of stone, more desirable than pure gold; for on them were engraved the sacred principles guiding them in the ways of faith in the unity of God and His spirituality—this at a time when all others sought to appease their deities according to their cruel practices. The sanctity of the family, founded upon reverence for parents, is the foundation of all society, and without which all is chaos and disorder. The relationship between man and his fellow is based on the admonition: "What is hateful to thee do not do unto thy fellow" [Tractate *Sabbath* 31a].

. . . If you continue to maintain this tradition, you too will be enabled to fulfill a noble role in the world, the role that so befits the descendants of the patriarchs, the offspring of those who heard the voices of the prophets. As you merit by your conduct, so will the nations honor you. Live your lives with generosity, with exalted thought and deed, for the betterment of mankind and for peace among nations.

Educate your children by the precepts which our fathers bequeathed us, which preserved our people and brought us to this day. Be faithful to your past and labor to perfect the world under the Kingdom of Heaven. The lamp which our ancestors conveyed to us will not pass away nor be lost over the generations. In this way will the Homeland flourish even though it remain small. In this way will the People of Israel live to fulfill its noble mission. It will take its place among the great nations, and the building blocks which it raises up in Eretz Yisrael will be strong and endure forever.

I have reached advanced age—to those years which, according to Ecclesiastes, "I have no pleasure in them" [Eccles. 12:1]. I have fulfilled my duty, "Because man goeth to his long home" [Eccles. 12:5]—and my eldest son James, who is of one mind with me, will further my work and will devote himself to the enterprise which I have begun.

May God protect the National Home in Eretz Yisrael!

Abraham Isaac Kook

Rabbi Kook (1865 – 1935) was the first Ashkenazic chief rabbi in modern Eretz Yisrael. He was a preeminent talmudic scholar and a prolific writer from an early age. His writings vibrate to a deep mystical chord and are permeated by a profound love of mankind. It is said of him that his main concern was the redemption of the Jewish people and of all mankind. Rabbi Kook was a leading spokesman of religious Zionism. After serving as rabbi in several Lithuanian cities, he came to Palestine in 1904 to be rabbi in Jaffa. After World War I he became rabbi of Jerusalem and in 1921 he was elected chief rabbi of Eretz Yisrael. He wrote the following will in 1919 when stricken with serious illness.

By the grace of God, Iyar 21, 5679 (1919), between the hours of nine and ten in the morning.

My hope is that God, in His mercy, will grant me a complete healing, among the other sick persons of His people Israel, and that in His abundant kindnesses He will enable me to return to Him in love. Especially do I pray that He enable me to mend whatever wrong I may have committed, whether in man's relationship to God or man's relationship to man, and that He grace me with the opportunity to repay my debts.

To my great regret I do not remember all my debts in detail. But I hope that God will bestir me and remind me of them all, and that He will help me to repay them. Some of those that have come to my mind I wrote down in a small notebook with a white cover, where there will also be found some poems. Some pages that were torn off from this notebook are with Zevi Yehuda [his son], may he be granted life, and some debts are also recorded there.

Most of the books in my apartment here do not belong to me. May God help me to return them to their owners. In my house in Jaffa too there are also many books that belong to others. May God enable me to clarify everything and to set everything in order.

May it be God's will to inspire whomever I may have pained or offended to forgive me with a full forgiveness. As for me, I surely forgive all. On the contrary, I regard as a good every pain and humiliation to which I was subjected. May it be God's will that no one suffer retribution on account of me, and may God bestow on all members of the fellowship of Israel only good and mercy.

O Lord, help me and heal me in Your abundant mercies, and strengthen me with Your help. Help Your holy people, and hasten the light of Your deliverance and establish Your holiness in all the worlds. Amen.

Resigned, yet anticipating Your help,
Abraham Isaac Hakohen Kook

My gold watch and chain is a gift of dear Shlesinger, may his memory be for a blessing, and I have some scruples about the gift. May God enable me to straighten it out properly, in accordance with the precepts of our holy Torah.

Ben Zion Meir Hai Uziel

Rabbi Uziel (1880 – 1953) was "Rishon LeZion," Sephardic chief rabbi of Eretz Yisrael. He was distinguished for his wisdom and for his efforts at reconciling all classes and elements of society and was universally beloved and respected. He was the author of a noteworthy volume of responsa, Mishpetei Uziel. *The following testament was written when he knew he had only two or three days to live following the amputation of a limb.*

In my role, I constantly kept before me as a lamp unto my feet these aims: to disseminate Torah among the students; to love the Torah and its commandments, the land of Israel and its sanctity; absolute love for every man and woman of Israel, for the entire peoplehood of Israel, and for the God of Israel; to implant peace among all men and women of Israel, in its body and soul, its speech and action, its thoughts and meditations,.its progress and exploits, at home and abroad, in town and city, to bring true peace into the household of Israel and its family, among the entire congregation of Israel in all its classes and factions, and between Israel and their Father in heaven. These latter two are actually one, since both emanate from one source, and that is *the Torah* of the living God, King of the universe, King of Israel and its holiness, who gave the Torah of Truth to His people; all whose ways are pleasantness and all whose paths are peace.

These two aims have been the ideal and the purpose of my life, and by them have I directed my path; and this prayer was on my lips each day: "Guide me by Thy counsel, lead me in Thy way, establish peace and truth among all Thy people Israel, to love and sanctify Thy name."

Certain it is that I have not succeeded even in the smallest measure to fulfill these goals which I set as my life's goal, but this I know—and the Almighty Who knows all secret things, knows—and all Israel knows that this was my intention and my prayer.

And now, as I take leave of you, my brethren and sisters, my teachers and mentors, all the House of Israel, to be gathered unto my fathers reposing in Eden, I thank you from the depths of my heart, collectively and individually, for honoring me in my lifetime beyond what my deeds and wisdom deserve, for the pleasantness with which you surrounded me by granting me a generous and substantial income with which to support myself and raise my family, may God preserve them, Amen.

I herewith ask your forgiveness and full pardon for any sins or offenses, slights or affronts I may have committed against any group or individual and failed to conciliate during my lifetime; if so, know and believe that it was unintentional. For the honor and wishes of every Jewish man and woman are the most precious and beloved to me of all public groups. But it is possible that as a mortal human being I may have caused someone, by accidental word or deed, some hurt or financial injury, and I hereby entreat you and say, forgive me and permit my soul to rest in peace.

Set aside all causes of separation and dispute from our midst and from our land, and establish in their stead all the elements for peace and unity, that our encampment may be pure, sanctified, fortified, and integrated, like a fortified barricade, against whom no destructive or vengeful force can be effectual. May God, Who maintains harmony in His celestial heights, cause peace for us and bless us according to His word by Moses His prophet:

> The Lord your God has multiplied you, and behold, you are this day as the stars of the heaven for multitude. The Lord God of your fathers make you a thousand times as many as you are, and bless you as He promised you. . . . The Lord will give strength to His people, the Lord will bless His people with peace. . . . And may the offering of Judah and Jerusalem be pleasant to the Lord as in the days of yore and years of old. [Deut. 1:10, 11; Ps. 29:11; Mal. 3:4]

Now I, your brother, take leave of you for life eternal, with blessings for peace, for the world's redemption with the establishment of the throne of the Davidian House, and for the rebuilding of God's sanctuary in Jerusalem, City of Holiness.

Alter Ya'akov Sahrai

Rabbi Alter Ya'akov Sahrai (1874 – 1937) was born in Poland where in his youth he studied under the Grand Rabbi Yehiel Ostrowski. He was an ardent Zionist and played an active role in the Mizrahi movement in its early stages of development. He settled in Eretz Yisrael in 1910, and served as communal secretary in Jerusalem for a number of years. He was a strong proponent of Jewish self-defense, and in his will he urges his children to defend those who cannot do so for themselves.

Written in Tel Aviv, Tamuz 13, 5693 [1933]

Praise and thanks do I give to the Creator of all and Master of the world for the soul He implanted and maintained within me, in His great kindness, all the years of my life. I did not expect that my frail body would endure to reach this age, but despite the many emotional crises, the physical infirmities, accidents, misfortunes, and the anguish of parenthood that I experienced, I survived, and by His will reached this point.

The days of my life have been days of sorrow and pain and not always have I been forbearing.

For forty years I have stood in the ranks of those laboring for the rebirth of our people and its land; and now, too, facing the end of my life, I maintain this view with all my might, and acknowledge the call to service incumbent upon every Jew who is loyal to his people, its Torah, and its land.

I address my children: I pray you, my dear ones, to remember that you are Jews, members of the Jewish nation, set apart from other nations and distinguished from them by virtue only of its Torah, that "Torah which Moses commanded us," and expounded by our sages in each generation.

A person who writes his will sees death before his eyes, whether it come now or after a time; and at this important time I say to you that the words of the Torah and of its expounders, the prophets and the sages of the Talmud, they are the guides who lead us to Divine Providence. Devote yourselves to constructive labors, to the task of physically rebuilding our land. It would be well if you affiliated with Mizrahi, Hapoel

Hamizrahi, or a similar group. Do not withdraw from any constructive work, particularly protecting the lives and property of the people of Israel in the Land of Israel. On the contrary, take your stand where those who are weaker and of a faint-hearted temperament are incapable of standing.

Meir Dizengoff

Meir Dizengoff (1861 – 1937) was the first mayor of Tel Aviv. He was born in Bessarabia where he was active in the Hovevei Zion movement, and he attended the early Zionist Congresses where he was strongly opposed to the Uganda Plan. In 1905 Dizengoff settled in Jaffa where he became a founder of the Ahuzat Bayit Company whose aim it was to establish a modern Jewish quarter near Jaffa. In 1921 the new quarter became the city of Tel Aviv and Dizengoff its first mayor, a post he held until his death except for the years 1925 – 1928. Before leaving for a rest cure in Jerusalem, he wrote a testament for publication upon his death. Shortly thereafter, on the day he died, the press carried the full text, portions of which appear here.

Tel Aviv, July 12, 1936

I should like my death to be by Divine Kiss. Is it not written that every man can be like Moses our teacher, and if he died thus, why not I? As a child, I imagined it in a plain and simple way: When Moses and the Israelites reached Mount Nebo, the Almighty Himself, in all His glory, came down to the mountain, called Moses to Him, and kissed him; and in that moment his soul fled. Later, after learning from my revered teachers that God has no bodily form or substance, I imagined the matter of death by Divine Kiss differently: On the summit of the mountain, from which one can see Jerusalem, the Dead Sea, and the land of the Jordan, God revealed Himself to Moses and said to him, " 'Enough, my servant Moses, you have accomplished much: You led the Israelites from Egypt, carried them through the wilderness, gave them the Torah, and brought them to the threshold of the Promised Land which I swore to give to them and their descendants as an eternal inheritance. Here is the land, a pleasant land, spread out before you; view it from the mountaintop, because your duty on earth is done. Ascend!' And Moses died; and no man knoweth the place of his sepulchre until this day" [Deut. 34:6]. This was death by Divine Kiss.

Viewed thus, many deaths may be seen as being by Divine Kiss. The last minutes in the life of Chief Rabbi Abraham Isaac Kook, of blessed memory, for example. As his expiration came near, his rabbinic comrades ringed his bed and prayed aloud, repeating the supreme declaration of every believing Jew, "Hear O Israel, the Lord our God, the Lord is One!" The dying rabbi responded to them in an ever-weakening voice, until at last, on the word "One" his soul fled. Now this was dying by Divine Kiss—because Harav Kook died calmly and contented, as one who had achieved the objectives of his lifetime. About such a person one may say, "The righteous live by their faith" (Hab. 2:4), and in their faith they die.

When I think about my own dying, the thought does not arouse in me any feeling of sorrow, morbidity, or sadness because this entire process of putting off one and putting on another aspect of existence is natural and normal. The time has come to conclude all the affairs of my life, my mundane activities; and I stand at the threshold of a new period and of a new world, far beyond me, on the other side of Awareness. The roles I have filled during my lifetime are satisfying, in that I did not spend my years for naught, and in that all my communal endeavors were for the benefit of my people and for the good of our beloved land.

I visualize my last day [on earth] as follows: After my bier will walk the children of Tel Aviv—those angels, those cherubs whom I loved so much all my days. In solid ranks, with heads held high, they follow behind my bier. And I can hear these youngsters' voices as they cry, "Don't leave us, dear grandfather; we love you dearly!"

Behind the children march the stalwart youth groups before whom are open unlimited opportunities in the tasks of liberty and redemption, and who live in an environment of dreams and idealistic strivings. I have always considered myself a friend to this younger generation and there has existed between us always a close spiritual bond. Whenever anyone asked me my age, I would reply, "I don't know precisely the number of years I have lived, but I feel ready for any daring, fantastic initiative, so long as it is worthwhile and leads to an ultimate goal." These youth will inherit our place and will lead us to the realization of our national strivings. It should be no wonder then that these youth accompany me to my final rest and that I rejoice within me over the fact; because even when I am on the other side of Awareness I shall maintain contact with these daring youth.

Next comes a large contingent of women who take part in the funeral. These are the mothers who gave birth to the young generation and who guard the chain of tradition linking the forefathers and their children. . . .

When they lower my body into the cold, damp grave and cover the bier with layers of earth, it seems to me that as a consequence of the great demonstration of the funeral procession, rays of light will break forth to penetrate the clumps of earth and illuminate the new journey on which I am bound, and to tell me that my death is not forced upon me but rather is by Divine Kiss.

Pinhas Rutenberg

Ukrainian-born Pinhas Rutenberg (1879–1942), engineer and revolutionary, arrived in Palestine in 1919. That same year he led a survey of the water resources with the view toward developing much-needed electric power, and in 1923 he organized the Palestine Electric Company. During his years as a pioneering force in Palestine's industrial development he also headed the Va'ad Leumi (National Council) three separate times, and worked with others in seeking a program for Arab-Jewish understanding. Rutenberg organized Jewish self-defense in Jerusalem in 1920 and headed the Hagganah in Tel Aviv. He bequeathed his estate to benefit youth programs; just prior to his death, he issued a call to Jewish youth for national unity, from which the following is an excerpt.

The division of our people into classes, communities, and parties has ever been an affliction. A civil war has brought us to the verge of destruction, and if it does not cease it will destroy us.

Therefore I beg and enjoin the community and the youth growing up in it to remember always that it is not as Jews of this class or that party that we are persecuted and slaughtered, but as the people of Israel as a whole.

Whether we like it or not we are brothers in suffering; let us understand this, and let us be brothers in living, in creating, for activity and building.

Our youth—the hope of our future, given its proper education—is the assurance of our continuity. The bases of its proper education are: rootedness, wisdom and knowledge, unity and brotherhood, earnestness and loyalty. To the education of youth in this spirit I dedicate the income of all my holdings, which has been and will be conveyed annually to the Pinhas Rutenberg Trust. May this capital and its incomes serve as the beginning of a fund for educating youth in the spirit of unity and brotherhood—the spirit of Israel.

I ask that the executors of the trust carry out this desire of mine.

Naftali Swiatitsky

The will of Naftali Swiatitsky is arresting on two counts: first, it describes the regrets of an aged father over a sin of omission committed many years earlier against one of his children and steps taken to amend the wrong; and second, it calls for the wronged son to return to Eretz Yisrael in order to claim his patrimony. Between the lines of this unusual will, ostensibly dealing with material bequests alone, we read a fuller story of a father seeking to reunite a son with his family and, simultaneously, with his brethren in the Jewish Homeland. Naftali Swiatitsky came to Petakh Tikva, "Mother of the Colonies," from Russia during the past century as one of the early pioneers. He was born in 1849 and died in Petakh Tikva in 1949.

Petakh Tikva
October 25, 1945
Heshvan 18, 5706

Because no one knows the exact time of his death and I am now already up in years when "I have no pleasure in them" [Eccles. 12:1]; being now ninety-five years of age, although I am still alert in my senses and I can walk with a cane on my own feet,

and since I have no tangibles or valuables or real estate to leave my children after me, since whatever I had from my labors during my years on earth I have already distributed among my children and I have no more to bequeath them,

now, before I go and am no more, and while I am still on my feet, normal in sense and limb, a certain realization picks at my mind like a mosquito, namely, that toward one of my sons—Mr. Gershon Swiatitsky, now forty years in America, in the city of Chicago, and who is called George Sweet—I have not properly fulfilled the duty of a father to his son.

This son left my home in Petakh Tikva forty years ago, and when he left he borrowed a sum of fifty or more francs, the coin of the realm at that time. This sum I have not been repaid by him till now, and in the meantime I have divided my properties among my three other children, while to my son Gershon Swiatitsky, who resides in the United States and is called George Sweet, I gave nothing because he was "out of sight, out of mind," as the saying goes.

Now, as I stand at the sunset of my life, I cannot forgive myself for the injustice with which I treated my son Gershon who is in America; and inasmuch as I myself own nothing today, neither movable nor real property, and can therefore bequeath him nothing whatever of my own, I have made a careful computation of the assets which I distributed earlier among my other children and divided it into four parts. The results indicate that I gave of Gershon's (called George) share to my other children in the following amounts: (1) To my son David, I gave 150 pounds; to my son Arieh, 150 pounds; to my daughter Mrs. Shifra Zimirovsky, 420 pounds, all appraised in terms of money values current at that time in Eretz Yisrael. By all rights it comes out that Gershon Swiatitsky (George Sweet) is owed 750 pounds from the properties that I gave my children during my lifetime.

It remains only for me to address my above-named two sons and daughter and to convey this as a final request. [I do this] in order that I may depart this world of vanities with the feeling that I have done my duty toward all four of my children and that I may not be ashamed, when I stand before the heavenly tribunal, over the unwarranted discrimination which I directed against my above-named son, George (whom I have not seen for forty years and whom I doubt I shall ever see again during my lifetime), in dividing what little I had in my power to give my heirs. I therefore instruct my three above-named children, David, Arieh, and Shifra, as a deed of final reverence for a parent, to consider themselves duty-bound to pay their brother Gershon Swiatitsky, known as George Sweet, whenever their brother comes to Eretz Yisrael, the amounts I have set, in cash, immediately upon his arrival in Eretz Yisrael. Let this be done immediately upon his arrival without hesitation, vacillation, or bargaining whatever. This is my last request of my children who received my property years ago, whose value has increased many-fold since then, and I instruct them to fulfill my request exactly as in this will.

I trust that my children will carry out this request faithfully and precisely so that I will not be ashamed of them when I come before the

Judge on high, before Whom are revealed the ways of all men and Who repays men according to their deeds [Jer. 17:10].

I have no other requests of my children. I pray they may attain long life, to ripe old age in joy; and may the Almighty grant them strength and wealth many times over what I was able to give them of my hard work over many years, and may they derive much pleasure from their own offspring.

The text of this will I sign in the presence of the chief rabbinate of Petakh Tikva and its environs, in the office of the chief rabbi of Petakh Tikva, Rabbi Reuven Katz, and I deposit in their care for safekeeping the original of this document with the requests that at my demise the above be brought to the attention of my children, to fulfill all the above; and a copy of this will be given to each of my four children so they may be informed exactly what the final request of my life is.

Not an elaborate funeral nor a beautiful tombstone, no pomp or honor—this I leave to the judgment of my children alone. I have only the one request which I have detailed above, simple and unambiguous, which I ask them to fulfill exactly, and I hope they will do so. Then I shall truly be able to rest in peace when my time comes; then shall I be an advocate on their behalf in the next world. All this have I set forth above. It is the sole request I make of my children.

Abba Berdiczew

Abba Berdiczew ("Berditchev") was among the Jewish men and women in Palestine who volunteered to parachute into German-occupied Europe in order to help Jews escape the Nazis. Berdiczew was parachuted into Slovakia, the land of his birth, and he met his death there. In his honor, a settlement in Israel's Lower Galilee is named Allonei Abba ("Oaks of Abba"). Many of its settlers are Holocaust survivors, some from Berdiczew's native Slovakia. He wrote the following testament before leaving on his final mission.

As the son of a tragic people that has paid the highest price in this war, my conscience impels me to sacrifice my all for its sake, even my very life. It is possible that the mission I have taken on myself is beyond my capacity. It is possible that I will not succeed even to begin fulfilling what has been entrusted to me; but I may not refuse. I may not even hesitate: because in the very places I left three years ago, thousands and tens of thousands of Jews are being killed, their homes destroyed, as they are erased from the face of the earth; because the fugitives of the sword are wanderers seeking a safe shore, and there is none; because thousands are daily seized by the Gestapo, burned, murdered in most brutal ways, imprisoned, and destroyed in systematic fashion; because in the Hell of Destruction they await impatiently a ray of light, a helping hand; because only by chance am I here, enjoying freedom and serenity.

Many yearn to be in my present condition, and only the higher politics of our "democratic" world has made them into sacrificial offerings.

Hannah Senesh

Hannah Senesh (1921 – 1944) immigrated to Palestine from her native Hungary just before the outbreak of World War II. She volunteered for the parachute corps and was dropped behind Nazi lines to work with partisan forces. She was captured by the Nazis, and after months of imprisonment and torture was executed in 1944. In addition to a legacy of heroism, Hannah Senesh left a collection of poems and a personal journal that reveal a gifted, sensitive spirit. She wrote this letter in December 1943, and arranged to have it given to her brother upon his arrival in Palestine should she fail to return from her mission. As it happened, he arrived the day before her departure. He was able to read the letter, then return it to her for security reasons.

Haifa
December 25, 1943

Darling George!

Sometimes one writes letters one does not intend sending. Letters one must write without asking oneself, "I wonder whether this will ever reach its destination."

Day after tomorrow I am starting something new. Perhaps it's madness. Perhaps it's fantastic. Perhaps it is dangerous. Perhaps one in a hundred—or one in a thousand—pays with his life. Perhaps with less than his life, perhaps with more. Don't ask questions. You'll eventually know what it's about.

George, I must explain something to you. I must exonerate myself. I must prepare myself for that moment when you arrive inside the frontiers of the Land, waiting for that moment when, after six years, we will meet again, and you will ask, "Where is she?" and they'll abruptly answer, "She's not here."

I wonder, will you understand? I wonder, will you believe that it is more than a childish wish for adventure, more than youthful romanticism that attracted me? I wonder, will you feel that I could not do otherwise, that this was something I had to do?

There are events without which one's life becomes unimportant, a worthless toy; and there are times when one is commanded to do something, even at the price of one's life.

I'm afraid, George, that feelings turn into empty phrases even though they are so impassioned before they turn into words. I don't know whether you'll sense the doubt, the conflicts, and after every struggle the renewed decision.

It is difficult because I am alone. If I had someone with whom I could talk freely, uninhibitedly—if only the entire burden were not mine, if only I could talk to you. If there is anyone who would understand me, I think you would be that one. But who knows . . . six years is a long time.

But enough about myself. Perhaps I have already said too much. I would like to tell you a few things about the new life, the new home, as I see them. I don't want to influence you. You'll see for yourself what the country is. But I want to tell you how I see it.

First of all—I love it. I love its hundred faces, its hundred climates, its many-faceted life. I love the old and the new in it; I love it because it is ours. No, not ours, but because we can make ourselves believe it is ours.

And I respect it. Not everything. I respect the people who believe in something, respect their idealistic struggle with the daily realities. I respect those who don't live just for the moment, or for money. And I think there are more such people here than anywhere else on earth. And finally, I think that this is the only solution for us, and for this reason I don't doubt its future, though I think it will be very difficult and combative.

As far as the kibbutz is concerned, I don't think it is perfect, and it will probably pass through many phases. But in today's circumstances it best suits our aims, and is the closest to our concept of a way of life—about this I have absolutely no doubt.

We have need of one thing: people who are brave and without prejudices, who are not robots, who want to think for themselves and not accept outmoded ideas. It is easy to place laws in the hands of man, to tell him to live by them. It is more difficult to follow those laws. But most difficult of all is to impose laws upon oneself, while being constantly self-analytical and self-vigilant. I think this is the highest form of law enforcement, and at the same time the only just form. And this form of law can only build a new, contented life.

I often ask myself what the fate of the kibbutz will be when the magic and novelty of construction and creation wear off, when the struggle for existence assumes reality and—according to plan—becomes an organized, abundant communal life. What will the incentive of the people be, what will fill their lives? I don't know the answer. But that day is so far in the future that it is best to think of existing matters.

Don't think I see everything through rose-colored glasses. My faith is a subjective matter, and not the result of outer conditions. I see the difficulties clearly, both inside and out. But I see the good side, and above all, as I said before, I think this is the only way.

I did not write about something that constantly preoccupies my thoughts: Mother. I can't.

Enough of this letter. I hope you will never receive it. But if you do, only after we have met.

And if it should be otherwise, George dear, I embrace you with everlasting love.

Your sister

P.S. I wrote the letter at the beginning of the parachute training course.

Enzo Hayyim Sereni

*Enzo Sereni (1905–1944), a member of a distinguished Italian family, im-
migrated to Palestine in 1927. He was active in the Histadrut, in the Mapai
party, and was among the founders of Givat Brenner, the settlement which
included among its members David Ben Gurion and Berl Katznelson. Sereni
felt, with others, that war in Europe was inevitable, and he went to Germany
and several other European countries between 1931 and 1934 to train Jewish
youth for settlement in Palestine. During World War II he served in the British
army, editing newspapers and broadcasting in Italian. Later he helped train
groups of parachutists to drop behind enemy lines to rescue Jews. He was
captured by the Germans in Italy and was shot in Dachau on November 18,
1944. His last message to his family is excerpted here.*

Greetings, children!

This afternoon we face our first parachute jump. Tomorrow we jump
twice, and day-after-tomorrow once more. After that we are real parachutists and can test our luck in practical endeavor. I feel well, calm,
even though, naturally, the first jump arouses some strange thoughts
and is a bit worrisome. One never knows how things will turn out and
whether he will pass the test. Till now, in the training program leading
up to the parachuting, I made it, more or less, although I am "an old man
among youth" around here. In the future, too, I hope that I may be
sustained by your merit and my luck.

Nonetheless at this moment before going out to "the test," I thought it
necessary to write to you. If anything should happen to me and I am
unable to see you again in this life, I want you to know that at this
moment I thought about you, about mother and grandmother, as the
most precious of all that I have in life. Parting from you this time was
difficult; each year my bond with grandmother grows stronger, as does
my love for mother and my loving solicitude for you. I want you to
become all that we have not succeeded in becoming: well-integrated,
normal, Jewish working people. And I also desire that you know how to
preserve the burning zeal and persistence that brought us—mother and
me—to the Land and to the pioneering movement, and that brought me,

in fact, to my present situation here. For I have believed from the first day that we Jews must actively participate in this war. I have tried to fulfill my duty to the best of my ability and have striven hard for this chance to demonstrate what a Jew can do. I have committed myself to this decision, and I consider it a correct one to this day.

I hope that we will see each other again, that not only following this test but following the practical tasks that come after it I will return to you. If I do not, care for your mother, care for grandmother, study, and remain true to yourselves and to me.

Once again, farewell to all of you, farewell to Givat Brenner for whose sake and in whose behalf I am here, and farewell to Eretz Yisrael. For, away from it, you are aware even more that you belong entirely to it; all else is just so much foam on the surface of the water.

Yours, with much love,
Father

Noam Grossman

The months between November 1947 when the U.N. resolution for partition had been achieved and May 15, 1948, the date of the establishment of the State of Israel, were fraught with danger for the Yishuv, the Jewish settlement in Palestine. The defense of the Yishuv was organized and carried out clandestinely and was poorly armed due to prevailing regulations of the British Mandate authority. Some pitched battles were fought and many Arab ambushes were repelled by self-sacrificing young men and women. Noam Grossman was one of these. His will, written January 12, 1948, was delivered inside a small envelope on which was written "To be opened only after I die."

This will of mine is written hurriedly without the opportunity for a farewell, even in a letter:

1. Bury me in Nahlat Yitzhak, Tel Aviv.

2. No need to write anything about me in the paper.

3. With my salary and any insurance my family receives—set up a fund for buying guns for the Irgun.

4. Return all my personal belongings to my family.

5. Do not eulogize me; I did my duty!

Avraham Kreizman

Chicago-born Avraham Kreizman came to Eretz Yisrael in 1921. Avraham fell in the War of Independence, alone, hurling hand grenades to protect the withdrawal of his friends. He left a wife and two young daughters. Here, three days before his death, he writes to his wife.

I know: When I die, for you I shall continue to live. No one will take me from your faithful and tender heart. But if you meet a comrade who understands your sorrow, and you love him a bit and your life brings forth a new life and a son is born to you—give him and let him carry my name and let him be my continuation.

And if it comes to pass that he does not understand—leave him without pain and let the child be our son alone. . . .

And when it comes to pass that a new settlement is built here, come and plant poppies in this place; they grow so beautifully here and thrive so well! And let this be the place of my grave. . . .

And perhaps you will err and your flowers will not be planted on my grave but on that of one of my comrades nearby. Well . . . another wife will think of her husband as she plants flowers on mine.

No one will be overlooked. Because we lie close to each other in this spot and there is no space here to divide a man and his friends. . . .

Eldad Pan

Eldad Pan was killed in Israel's War of Independence at the age of twenty, a veteran of many battles. The translation from the original Hebrew is by Sidney Greenberg.

Lately I have been thinking about what the goal of life should be. At best, man's life is short. His life may be kind or harsh, easy or difficult, but the time passes before he realizes it. An old person wants to live no less than a young person. The years of life do not satisfy the hunger for life. What then shall we do during this time?

We can reach either of two conclusions. The first is that since life is so short we should enjoy it as much as possible. The second is that precisely because life is short and no one can completely enjoy it (for we die with half our desire unsatisfied) [*Eccles. Rabba* I, 2], therefore we should dedicate life to a sacred and worthy goal, to sacrifice it for something which will be valued above life. At times the first feeling is stronger and at others the second one. Of late, however, I think that the second feeling is dominant. It seems that I am slowly coming to the conclusion that life by itself is worth little unless it serves something greater than itself.

Dvora Waysman

Dvora Waysman is a distinguished writer in Israel who contributes articles and studies to the English language Jewish press in many countries. She and her family were olim, *settlers in modern Israel. The problems of migrating to a new land are many and, with young children, intensified. In her ethical will she speaks eloquently and poetically of her deep love for Israel and of her everlasting joy at her family's becoming part of the Land and its people.*

As I write this, I am sitting on my Jerusalem balcony, looking through a tracery of pine trees at the view along Rehov Ruppin. I can see the Knesset, the Israel Museum, and the Shrine of the Book—that architectural marvel resembling a woman's tilted breast, that houses the Dead Sea Scrolls.

I am at an age where I should write a will, but the disposition of my material possessions would take just a few lines. They do not amount to much . . . had we stayed in Australia where you—my four children—were born, they would be much more. I hope you won't blame me for this.

For now you are Israelis, and I have different things to leave you. I hope you will understand that they are more valuable than money in the bank, stocks and bonds, and plots of land, for no one can ever take them away from you.

I am leaving you the fragrance of a Jerusalem morning . . . unforgettable perfume of thyme, sage, and rosemary that wafts down from the Judean hills. The heartbreaking sunsets that give way to Jerusalem at night . . . splashes of gold on black velvet darkness. The feel of Jerusalem stone, ancient and mellow, in the buildings that surround you. The piquant taste of humus, tehina, felafel—foods we never knew about before we came here to live.

I am leaving you an extended family—the whole house of Israel. They are your people. They will celebrate with you in joy, grieve with you in sorrow. You will argue with them, criticize them, and sometimes reject them (that's the way it is with families!). But underneath you will be proud of them and love them. More important, when you need them—they will be there!

I am leaving you the faith of your forefathers. Here, no one will ever laugh at your beliefs, call you "Jew" as an insult. You, my sons, can wear *kippot* and *tzitzit* if you so wish; you, my daughters, can modestly cover your hair after marriage if that is what you decide. No one will ridicule you. You can be as religious or as secular as you wish, knowing it is based on your own convictions, and not because of what the "goyim" might say. You have your heritage . . . written with the blood of your people through countless generations. Guard it well and cherish it—it is priceless!

I am leaving you pride. Hold your head high. This is your country, your birthright. Try to do your share to enhance its image. It may call for sacrifice, but it will be worth it. Your children, their children, and all who come after, will thank you for it.

I am leaving you memories. Some are sad . . . the early struggles to adapt to a new country, a new language, a new culture. But remember, too, the triumphs . . . the feeling of achievement when you were accepted, when "they" became "us." That is worth more than silver trophies and gold medals. You did it alone—you "made" it.

And so, my children, I have only one last bequest. I leave you my love and my blessing. I hope you will never again need to say: "Next year in Jerusalem." You are already there—how rich you are!

Part Four

WILLS OF MODERN AND CONTEMPORARY AMERICAN JEWS

In this section we read some of the wills that document how parents have tried to convey the tradition to children growing up in America. The New World has been a place of hope for Jews, a synonym for opportunity. But life in America has also been a challenge, for American life offers choices. Some of the options threaten to supplant tradition and others tend to weaken the links between the generations.

It is not surprising that these American wills differ from the traditional ones; time and place have altered even the language in which they are written. The traditional values are not emphasized in these pages as often as in the earlier wills. Instead, the urgency here underlies exhortations to group survival and to family fidelity.

But these ethical wills share with those of all the ages two common characteristics: One is optimistic hope for the individual and collective future. The other is a palpable seriousness; for the prospect of death, even the dim awareness of its ultimate reality, imbues one's thoughts with an edge of gravity.

Emil Greenberg

Emil Greenberg's will contains a rare combination of literary style of high quality with fervent devotion to the Jewish heritage and its continuity. After a brief introduction to ethical wills, the writer lucidly sets forth his "legacy of intangibles."

Dated, this 59th birthday,
the 15th day of February, 1965

The ancient Hebrew tradition of an ethical will, "a legacy of intangibles" as characterized by Stephen Vincent Benet, has regrettably fallen into disuse. I presume that it is a matter of values. The monies and properties, the tangible assets we bequeath, have solid, corporeal, material value and in these hurtling times what are the real values of *Pirke Avot,* the ethics of our fathers?

Nevertheless an anachronistic but stubbornly persisting insight and foresight impel me to give, devise, and bequeath unto my progeny and perhaps to their progeny the conscious presence of a sense of ethics, a continuity and tradition of a way of life.

So here we take inventory of precept instead of property, of concern instead of cash, of love in lieu of legacy. I am humbly grateful that this inventory includes such great contributions from your family forebears.

It is no smugness that evaluates the unassuming goodness of my mother and the twinkling kindliness of my father. But the inheritance they left was more than pervading goodness; they handed down a great hunger, a hunger for knowing, for inquiring, for helping, a many-faceted hunger. I earnestly believe they handed down to their sons their encompassing concern for everyone in every station of life, augmented by the opportunities afforded by that education in the professions for which they strove so indomitably. Complete financial disaster was just an obstacle, never a deterrent.

So the family tradition of love for learning which an unschooled mother had inculcated so well, I would that I could too.

It is also in our Hebrew tradition, the choice of a people who chose the book instead of the brand, the Torah, not terror. But even learning can become sophistry. It would be the greatest of ironies if the ceaseless search for knowledge were to find its goal in submergence under the smothering quicksand of conversion and conformity. The threat of obliteration is urgently real and deadly.

When you wonder why you are and should remain Jews throughout the generations, always remember as your heritage, millennia-old, the unbroken continuity and tradition literally paid for in blood and torture, pogrom and Bergen-Belsen. It isn't just an unbroken chain, it is a lifeline. However, you cannot just feel it, you must also know it; study it and you must share identity with every Jew who ever suffered and died for *kiddush ha-Shem.*

Lives are not always grand nor are they epic. We interweave vignettes of small-talk, little gestures, minor favors, and family folkways so that we do not live alone within our solitary selves. No people are all bad or all good. When you degrade or derogate others, your own stature is correspondingly lessened.

Seek graciousness. It is the lubrication of civilized life; it makes the essential harshness and ruthlessness and crudity of Truth easier to live with, when it cannot be solely lived for. However, you should also remember that graciousness is a way *to* life, but not by itself a way *of* life.

Here your Hebrew heritage becomes manifest. Other civilizations— the Sumerian, the Chaldean, the Babylonian, the Egyptian, the Hellenic, the Roman—were cultured and grandiose, hedonistic and amoral. It was the ethical gadfly of your irritant, uncompromising Hebrew ancestor-prophets which gave high purpose and meaningfulness to Civilization and its cultures.

In our present fabulous era of wondrous change and achievement each little ego becomes literally overwhelmed. Without fundamental guidelines and basic roots in a family heritage, each of us, in the words of Clarence Darrow, "is not the captain of his soul and the master of his fate, he is just a hapless deckhand on a rudderless raft aimlessly adrift in a limitless sea."

If I can bequeath something of my concept of mores and aspirations, distilled of its inevitable portion of baseness and frailty, so that my children and their issue may partake in some measure of high hope and heritage, to that degree a wisp, a whisper of immortality becomes mine, and yours.

Liebman Adler

Rabbi Liebman Adler (1812 – 1892) was an early spiritual leader of Chicago's first synagogue, Kehillat Anshe Ma'arav, established in 1847. He served as K.A.M.'s rabbi from 1861 until his death. An outspoken critic of slavery, Rabbi Adler's sermons stressed that God-fearing people had a duty to put an end to this great wrong. He disliked pomp of any kind, including oratorical displays that obscure the full meaning in sermons. Thus, despite his great erudition, Adler always translated his knowledge into terms which the average listener could understand. A history of the K.A.M. (1951) states that all who knew him "acknowledged reverence for the sterling integrity of the man."

My Last Will

I desire that there be no haste in my interment. If there are no signs of decomposition sooner, the funeral should not be until forty-eight hours after my death.

If the physician who treated me should find it desirable in the interest of science to hold a postmortem examination, I would like that he be not interfered with.

My coffin shall not cost more than $7.

No flowers.

My funeral to be directly from the place of demise to the cemetery.

No funeral oration.

Dear Hannah: In view of your delicate health, I desire that you remain at home and not join the funeral if the weather is the least inclement.

Not more than three days' mourning in domestic retirement.

I cherish the kaddisch [sic]—prayers of mourning in the synagogue— of my sons and daughters as it deserves, but I do so only if you, after the expiration of the year of mourning, do not omit attendance at the synagogue without necessity.

If financial conditions permit, each of my married children should join a Jewish congregation, the fittest being the K.A.M.—Kehillath Anshe Maarabh [Ma'arav], "Congregation of the Men of the West," corner of Indiana Avenue and Thirty-third Street.

Those children who do not live too distant should, if the weather permit, and if it can be done without disturbing their own domestic relations, gather every Friday around the mother.

My children, hold together. In this let no sacrifice be too great to assist each other and to uphold brotherly and sisterly sentiment. Each deed of love you do to one another will be balm to my soul. The example of eleven children of one father who stand together in love and trust would be to his grave a better decoration than the most magnificent wreath of flowers, which I willingly decline, but leave to your judgment.

The small savings which I leave will come to you only after the death of the mother. I know you; I may trust that you will not meet in an unfilial way about possession and disposition. The heritage which is already yours is a good name and as good an education as I could afford to give. It does not look as if any of you had a disposition to grow rich. Do not be worried about it. Remain strictly honest, truthful, industrious, and frugal. Do not speculate. No blessing rests upon it even if it be successful. Throw your whole energy into the pursuance of the calling you have chosen. Serve the Lord and keep Him always before you; toward men be amiable, accommodating, and modest, and you will fare well even without riches. My last word to you is: Honor your mother. Help her bear her dreary widowhood. Leave her undisturbed in the use of the small estate, and assist if there should be want.

Farewell, wife and children!

Another point, children. I know well you could not, if you would, practice Judaism according to my views and as I practiced it. But remain Jews and live as Jews in the best manner of your time, not only for yourself, but also where it is meet to further the whole.

Yitschak Kelman

Rabbi Yitschak Kelman was born in Galicia in 1867. He was descended from a long line of scholars and rabbis, and he continued the family tradition. After serving as rabbi in several Eastern European communities and in Vienna, he came to America to serve as rabbi in Jamaica, Queens, at the invitation of countrymen who had settled there. Despite the suffering he and his family experienced in Europe, he remained a kind and warm person and earned the affection of his people by his piety, learning, devotion to the Law, and his many deeds of loving-kindness. Because of his fairness and love of peace, he was often called on to arbitrate disputes. Although he did not write for publication, his studies, sermons, and notes have been gathered by his family and published in a volume, Moreshet Avot, *from which this will is taken and translated. Rabbi Kelman died in 1933.*

These are my instructions as to what is to be done for me in my time of illness and from the time of my death until after the burial. Since a person is not always in full possession of his faculties then, I set these requests down now:

1. People should visit frequently so that when the final time comes there will be a minyan present.

2. I should be reminded to recite the confessional, and before this to give charity in accordance with my means.

3. I should be reminded to repent and to recite *Adon Olam* and *Yigdal* for they contain the thirteen essential principles of faith which a person must believe.

4. The book *Shevet Musar* should be brought, or Reb Feival Sfard of Zlotnick should be asked to bring the fourteenth section of *Sde Hemed* in which the text of the declaration of intention is found. A minyan of pious and observant Jews should be brought into the room so that I may recite the declaration in their presence.

5. Then I should be given the book *Ma'avar Yabok* and together with the quorum of ten Jews let me recite what is written there.

6. If it is known that I am on bad terms with anyone, I should be reminded of this so that I can forgive him. And if it is known that anyone is on bad terms with me, he should be requested to forgive me. I ask that

it be anounced in the synagogue that I forgive any and everyone who may have aggravated me and that I ask any and everyone whom I may have aggravated to please forgive me.

7. Let ten pious and observant Jews say Psalms on my behalf and let a prayer for my recovery be recited with my name and the name of my mother, and let charity on my behalf be given to the fund that is named for Rabbi Meir Ba'al Hanes in the Holy Land, and let that charity be placed in the charity box of that fund promptly. If funds are available let them be distributed to poor scholars and to ordinary poor Jews, and if money is not available then let the best clothes or the watch or books be sold and the money given to charity, both before and after my going. It is best to do these things in the morning after the prayers, for this is a time of mercy and a favorable moment.

8. Before the prayers and the giving of the charity one of the ten should say a word of instruction to the people reminding them that they should realize and repent, and asking them to learn a lesson from what is happening. He should ask them to pray for me, both in this world and after my departure, that no harm should come to me.

9. The Holy Presence is with the sick. Therefore my family should be reminded to keep the sickroom and the house clean and pure as if a king were coming. And I too should be kept clean. This is a part of human dignity, so that those who come to visit the sick should not feel any discomfort, as it is written: "Let your camp be holy for the Lord is in your midst" (Deut. 23:15). Let there be a fresh sheet and a fresh garment regularly.

10. You should be very careful to see to it that I do not neglect any commandment which a well person is required to fulfill. For example, when I am given food to eat or water to drink, I should be reminded to say the appropriate blessing, and I should be reminded to wash before I say the blessing, as it is written: "I will wash my hands in cleanliness" (Pss. 26:6, 73:13).

At the Time of Death

The sages have taught that it is a good deed to be present at the time of death, and that this takes precedence even over prayer. Therefore there ought to be many people present at such a time so that they can divide into two groups, one to pray, the other to stand by the sick person's side. They should say Psalms and study Mishnah and do those things that are prescribed in the *Ma'avar Yabok*. (My copy can be found in the section of my library where the booklets are kept.)

The soul is pleased when relatives are nearby at the time of death, but only if they do not wail. Therefore only those men who know they will not break down should be there. Women should not be allowed in for it is their nature to weep uncontrollably.

The children should be kept away from the time of dying until the time to say kaddish at the grave. . . .

Since a person is not always in full possession of his faculties at the end there is the danger that he may deny his faith. Therefore it is important that at this time he say: "Hear O Israel, the Lord our God, the Lord is One," and take upon himself the yoke of the kingdom of heaven.

In case that I am not lucid at the end I hereby authorize my closest friends to recite the declaration of intent for me, and I hereby declare this authorization to be noncancellable. The text can be found on page 12 of the *Ma'avar Yabok*. It begins with the phrase: "My brothers, my friends, and my teachers."

When the Soul Separates from the Body

If possible let me be attended by those who have purified themselves in the *mikvah* that day. . . .

Let there be no eulogies for me, but if someone knows something good that I have done they may mention it. And let no one say anything derogatory for it is surely forbidden to speak badly of the dead.

Before the purification and the washing let charity be given in an amount equal to the numerical value of my name, and again when my body is put into the coffin let this be done again.

Let this be the contents of the announcement that appears in the newspaper after my death:

On such and such a day, in the week of such and such Torah portion, on such and such day of the month, Rabbi Isaac, the son of

Mirel, who was once rabbi in Wizniowczyk and for one year in Podhorvyze and then here in Jamaica, in America, departed this life. His friends and his students, wherever they may be, are requested to study Mishnah for the first month, and especially for the first week, and to say that they do this for his sake, and let them make mention of any good quality of his to which they can testify such as loving-kindnesses that I did for many people.

Whatever rituals are performed out of respect to the living may be done after me, but let there not be any praise that is not true, for this is a great detriment to the soul.

Immediately after the week of mourning let a tombstone be erected, or at least by the end of the first thirty days, for according to the *Zohar,* the soul yearns for the body and craves to at least know where it rests.

1. Even though I have said above that I want no eulogy, if there are any rabbis present at the funeral they may say a few short words of comfort to the mourners and teach those present a lesson in how to live if they wish, but if so please let them not be too long.

2. Let there be only pious observant Jews who put my body in the grave. I ask that they break the bottom of the coffin so that the body rests directly on the earth. This is what I did for my father, my teacher, may his soul be in heaven.

3. I ask that the washing be done in the *mikvah* of my dear friend, Reb Avraham Reizman, but only if my death should occur on a weekday. But if it should be on the eve of the Sabbath, especially if it is in winter when the days are very short, then let the washing be done as quickly and simply as possible so as not to lead, God forbid, to a desecration of the Sabbath. . . .

4. After the burial let charity be given to the poor once again in accordance with the numerical value of my name.

5. Let services be held all during the week of *shivah* in the room in which my soul expires and let a light be kept lit there all during that week. After services let several chapters of Psalms be said. If the people wish they may study a chapter of Mishnah every day. Each chapter should begin with a letter of my name.

I ask that a bit of earth from the Land of Israel be put into my grave. You will find the earth in a package which is in my dresser.

And know, my children, that you should show very great reverence for my helpmate. By doing this you will fulfill a double commandment— honoring her, and honoring me through honoring her. For it was she who kept me in health, for I was always a sickly person, and she kept me from sin as well. Therefore do not be ungrateful and do not aggravate her in any way in her old age. Show her reverence, please, just as I did for my mother, after the death of my father. I adorned her with glory and honor until her dying day. This is in keeping with the teaching of Rabbi Judah the Prince, whose last words at the time of his death were: 'Be careful of the honor of your mother." I know that it is enough to ask this of you just once. . . .

Bernard L. Levinthal

Head of the Orthodox rabbinate in Philadelphia, Rabbi Levinthal (1865 – 1952) was among the founders of the Union of Orthodox Rabbis of the United States and Canada and of the Mizrahi Organization of America. European-born Rabbi Levinthal had profound admiration for the American way of life and was deeply proud of the biblical roots of democracy. A son, Judge Louis E. Levinthal, told how his father used to take the family on Sabbath walks to Independence Hall and point out the biblical verse from the Book of Leviticus inscribed on the Liberty Bell.

My help is from the Lord, Creator of heaven and earth.

To my sons—long life be theirs:

I request of you, my dear sons, to strengthen yourselves and be punctilious in the retention and the observance of the commands of our holy Torah. Now in the matter of observing the law and commandments and living up to the *mitzvot* in practice, all of us, of course, continue to be bound by the oath taken at the foot of Mount Sinai. What I say here therefore refers more paticularly to such matters as require special care, namely, that you be watchful and solicitous in public and communal affairs so as not to cause, God forbid, the profanation of God's name and His Torah. Now in these matters there are degrees, so that personality has a chance to express itself.* Therefore please be very careful not to profane my name and the name of our fathers and the name of our family. Be careful not to participate in and waste your efforts on movements which are not to the advantage of traditional Torah, or on activities which go counter to efforts which I—with the help of God, blessed be His name—have made and to achievements for the strengthening of Torah and observance which I have nurtured and fostered with a sense of dedication rising from the very depths of my soul and for which I have sacrificed my very life. Each one of you should try, in accordance with his powers, to strengthen Traditional Judaism in this

*Literally, in connection with which the rabbis would say, "a person like me. . . ."

land of our habitation, and you will thereby merit participation in the life of the Torah in our Holy Land.

I am certain that my sons will—with God's favor—be careful to observe, during the days of mourning for me, everything which Jews accept as proper in the observance of the commandment to honor one's father after his term of life has ended. They must be careful indeed not to commit even the slightest transgression in connection with this. Every day of mourning for me they shall study a portion of the Bible, Mishnah, and Halakhah in whatever language they understand; and every day they shall give charity for my soul's elevation.

If, whenever my Creator, blessed be His name, wills it, my passing from this life occurs in our country, here in America, they shall bury me in the grave which I have fixed for myself here. I do not ask to be carried to the Holy Land, out of respect for the rabbis who preceded me and especially out of respect for my father-in-law, the Gaon, blessed be his memory, as well as out of respect for the pious and righteous laymen, peace be upon them, whose honored resting place is here and who worked together with me in all manner of sacred causes. If, however, my departure from life occurs, God forbid, outside of our country, I request that my sons carry me to the Holy Land; and I command my sons—long life be theirs—that in such a case they carry also the remains of the wife of my youth, peace be upon her, to the Holy Land in accordance with the condition which I made at the time of her burial.

I request that no adjectives be inscribed on my tombstone, other than "The well-known rabbi who labored at his sacred task so and so many years." I request also that those who eulogize me refrain from multiplying their praises of my learning and fear of God, but that they shall speak of my labor at my sacred task and of my activities and achievements in realizing the commandments of the Torah—perhaps this will be, with God's help, of my encouragement to others, and so add to my merits as well.

At the time of the funeral, and also during the period of eulogizing, the elder among the rabbis present—long life be his—shall three times, in my name, make announcement of my request for forgiveness by all those whom I may have caused, God forbid, some financial loss either as the result of an error in teaching or in judicial decision; as well as by those whom I may have pained by words uttered or otherwise harmed, knowingly or unknowingly. He shall ask that all these persons forgive me. I, for my part, forgive those who angered me or ever caused me shame or financial loss; I do so in the hope that they too will forgive me.

I request my sons—long life be theirs—to come together, if at all possible, on the day of my *yahrzeit* and discuss practical and spiritual matters concerning the realization of my requests in this my testament, as well as to heighten the sentiments of affection and brotherliness among themselves.

Also my sons—long life be theirs—shall at all times stand at one another's side in an hour of need, God forbid. They shall support a needy brother with good advice as well as with practical aid. This matter is an obligation and takes precedence over all other charities; for so our sages, may their memory be for a blessing, said: whichever (of the following) expressions precedes the other in the Bible takes precedence also in observance: "To thy brother; to thy poor; and to the needy in the land." . . .

To my daughter's son-in-law, the rabbi, the Gaon, Rabbi Samuel Belkin—long life be his—I advise that he make his Torah—the Torah of truth, the Torah of instruction and judgment—his wholehearted occupation. He will thus be a branch of our family, a family of rabbis, teachers, and leaders in Israel for many generations. And I have faith in God—blessed be His name—that his learning and his fear of God will stand by him, so that, with God's help, he will be a source of pride and glory and honor to us all.

Baruch Shapiro

Rabbi Baruch Shapiro of Mahzikei Hadat congregation in Seattle, Washington, makes an unusual request of the congregational leadership. After arranging bequests for relatives and bestowing generous gifts upon several dozen Torah institutions, Rabbi Shapiro makes unique provision for the future rabbinic leadership of his synagogue. This provision, excerpted from the will, appears below.

Sivan 12, 5722
June 14, 1962

After all the expenses for burial and any other expenses, all of my remaining assets I hereby bequeath entirely to our Mahzikei Hadat congregation in Seattle, Washington, for the purpose that they may elect and retain a rabbi, a great scholar of Talmud and Jewish jurisprudence, whose qualifications should be sanctioned by the three great scholars Rabbi Eliezer Silver, Rabbi Aaron Kotler, and Rabbi Moshe Feinstein. In accordance with the income of our Mahzikei Hadat congregation now they would not be able to afford this so they shall be permitted to use from these assets that I bequeath for this purpose up to 50% of the cost (to defray the expense of hiring and paying said rabbi) when needed.

The rabbi who will be retained after me will be in better circumstances than those in which I was because of different situations. With proper leadership of the congregation more members can be added. Also, the other congregations may begin to understand how important and necessary the English-speaking rabbis are and how good they may be; there must also be available a rabbi who is a great scholar of Talmud and Jewish jurisprudence, not only because of the honor of the Torah which is very necessary for Judaism, like air to breathe, but also to be able to determine the answers to all complicated questions that arise in this country even more than in the Old Home.

David De Sola Pool

Rabbi David De Sola Pool (1885 – 1970) was head of New York's Sephardic synagogue, Shearith Israel, the oldest synagogue in the United States. London-born Rabbi Pool was brought to New York in 1907 to lead Shearith Israel, and he held that position until his retirement in 1956. He wrote several books, including An Old Faith in the New World: Portrait of Shearith Israel, 1654 – 1954. *His many communal endeavors included his serving as president of the American Jewish Historical Society, representing the United States as delegate to the NATO Atlantic Congress in London in 1959, and as founder and a director of the Jewish Education Committee of New York.*

The end of the matter, all having been heard: revere God and keep His commandments; for this is the whole man.

—Ecclesiastes 12:13

Whensoever death shall come, it will find me unafraid. I pray that it may find me ready. I have ever tried so to live that I might be prepared to meet my God. I love life and the exquisite gifts of work, of play, of joy, of chastening, of light, of laughter, and most of all, of love that it has brought me. I am, and have always been, deeply grateful for the abundance of life with which I have been blessed. Life has been inexpressibly sweet to me. Yet, come death when it may, I yield up life as gladly, as gratefully, as I have accepted its gift for the while . . . it would be selfish to ask for more. All my life long I have been blessed with the gifts of love, far, far beyond my deserving. I have tried, haltingly, inadequately, but sincerely . . . to repay through service some of the debt I owe to life for its profuse bounty toward me. I gave three years (the happiest of my life because the richest in service) to the Holy Land. I have tried at all times, and for all who called upon me, rich as well as poor, gentile as well as Jew, to give service through such poor gifts as my physical strength, my mental power, and my spiritual resources enabled me to offer. I have tried so to do. More than that I cannot say, for I know that often, pitifully often, I have failed through weakness and inadequacy—physical, mental, and spiritual. Yet the stimulus and the joy of trying have been mine.

From anyone toward whom I have failed in human kindness I ask forgiveness. I do not feel, and I never have felt, any unkindness or malice in my heart toward anyone. Where I have failed, it has been through my insufficiency, never through ill-will.

But I would not leave with you who care to hear, and even perchance to cherish, a message from me any emphasis on failure. Though in tangible achievement I have not done what perhaps I dreamed of doing and what the world may rightly have expected me to achieve, the very living of my life has been supremely successful. There has been no day in which my heart has not leaped with gratitude to God for the joy of life and its fulfillment in the perfect love that has been given to me both as a child and in every moment of my sacred married life. There has yet never dawned the day when I have not been able to give thanks unto God for His goodness, and the day of death shall be but one more such day.

Therefore I would not have my death darken the life of anyone. Life to me has always been joy with humor and laughter and happiness. I would have it so, and I have tried to make it so for all others with whom my lot has been cast. I have tried to comfort others in their sorrow and to show them the sunshine of life's path. So if any would remember me, let my name be mentioned with a smile, with brightness, with humor, with happy memory, with wholesome gladness. Pain not my memory with tears or regrets, but let my spirit live among you after death as it has on earth, with joyousness. I would have the children of the religious school of my congregation gladdened on the Sunday nearest its anniversary or, should that be in the summer, then I would have some other children's lives made sweeter on that day, and at all times I would have my wife and children and those who have been the sweetest blessings in my life recall me with a smile as they think of how much heartwarming love they gave to me.

I can never even begin to express my thanks to all whose goodness, whose forbearance, and whose friendship have made my life so wondrous an adventure. May God bless you all for the blessings you have given to me. I have had all and more than man could dare ask for—a life that has known no want, a life of wide and varied interests, with music, travel, humor, work, opportunities of spiritual service. But most of all I have had friendship and kindness from everyone, and a perfect, exquisite love from my life's partner.

> Many waters cannot quench love
> Rivers cannot drown it. . . .

To those I have loved my message is contained in Eleanor Graham's sonnet:

> It is not for myself that I fear death. . . .
> Hear then my infinite conceit; I fear
> That those I love, who love me too, may heap
> Small portions of their lives upon my bier.
> Would there be tears and I not here to bring
> A cause for living laughter?
> Would there be darkness and pain, and I not here to sing
> Return of day? Oh, take this from me—
> Promise that when I'm one with all the after
> You still will greet each newborn day with laughter.

To all I would sum up what I have tried to be in the deep wisdom of the ancient words: "The end of it, when all has been heard, is revere God and keep His commandments, for this is the whole of man."
So,

> I rest my spirit in His hand,
> Asleep, awake by Him I'm stayed.
> God with me still, in life, in death,
> I face my future unafraid.

Gottlieb Wehle

This is the testament of Gottlieb Wehle, member of a group of Sabbatian families who settled in America in the late 1840s. According to the genealogy published by his son, Theodore Wehle, Gottlieb Wehle was born in Prague in 1802 and died in New York in 1881. He was the great-uncle of Justice Louis D. Brandeis and a first cousin of Zecharia Frankel, one of the founders of the Wissenschaft des Judentums *movement. This testament is unique in at least one respect, that is, it is the latest known testament written by a Jewish Sabbatian who avows belief in the basic tenets of Sabbatism. The following is a portion of the full text, translated from the German by Gershom Scholem.*

In the name of God, the Ruler of Human Destiny!

My dear, beloved children,

I start today a document, the commencement of which I put off for many years. With every year, however, it is more pressing. Alas, far too often the frailty of the human being becomes more evident, so that it eventually appears impossible to make arrangements which before would have been only too easy.

Every father of a family feels forced, on reaching a certain age, especially when tragic events occur in his family or kin, to realize that he also is not secure against a sudden recall from the stage; and that it is therefore advisable, as long as he commands ripe and mature sense, to convey to his children and relatives, with cool and clear mind, his last "Testament." In ordinary life this is known as "making his will," meaning the writing down of dispositions and arrangements by a wealthy father, directing how his personal and real estate are to be divided after his departure. But there are matters besides chattels and fortunes of which a father wishes to talk seriously to his children when departing this life.

It is well known to you, my dear children, that influenced by the repeated popular demonstrations in Prague against the Jews, I decided to leave the Continent, the country and the town where I and also you were born; where my ancestors throughout the centuries lived an honorable life agreeable to God; where they suffered innocently and so greatly for their belief and their nationality. It is not granted to me to share with them the clod of earth, where they rest in peace.

The pedigree of my parents has been known in Prague for centuries—all these ancestors were noted for their biblical and talmudical learning, for their practice of charity, their honest and blameless way of living, their wealth and inoffensiveness. These are only general traits, which may seem strange to you, as you are removed from those circles, where these gentle-folk have always been mentioned with the greatest respect. They were the dignitaries of Bohemian Jewry. Now your ancestors declared all the old and new writings concerning the Talmud as wrongly exploited by sophistical and astute commentators; that they were only the outer shell and peel of the true Judaism, which instead represented doctrines that were the quintessence and symbol of Judaism, higher than the discussions, debates, questions, and solutions of old and long-forgotten laws about offerings and food. In consequence your ancestors were decried as heretics by many hypocritical, so-called public educators. They were slandered and persecuted by them. These hypocrites dared even from the pulpit to stir up the people against them, under the pretext that the principles and doctrines of this "sect," as they called them, had much in common, even the same tendencies, as the Christians. They mesmerized the listeners, even publishing pamphlets containing the most impudent and gross calumnies, which were distributed with lightning speed throughout the greater part of Europe. Persecuted by these hypocrites and zealots, these "heretics, zoharites, and Sabbatians" endured the intolerance with gentle resignation, without asking the authorities for their proffered protection. Strangely enough, even the most fanatical opponents had to admit their high intelligence, blameless way of life, strict morality, honesty, and charity: in fact all the virtues of a good citizen.

With pious and gentle resignation the persecuted ones suffered this intolerance. They were moved by their resolve to establish the principles of revealed religion, its high purposes, and the future destiny of their nation. They gladly resigned their perfect knowledge of the Talmud because they were seeking the spirit of religion. They arranged their theological studies in the spirit of the Bible and various other old theological scriptures known under the generally ill-reputed name of Kabbalah. They placed higher the doctrines of this secret lore than the dead ceremonies, and tried to revive the spirit contained in them.

"That man, being an image and masterpiece of God, will again return to the perfect state, as he was when he left the Creator's hand; that he will be free from all sickness of body, mind, and soul; that he will be again innocent as before the Fall, free from vice and sin"—this was roughly the program of their endeavors and perception of God, the aim of their studies. Moreover, as God acts only indirectly, a chosen, consecrated Messiah is necessary as deputy of his highest Master. As now, acording to the Kabbalistic principles, man is only the tool of Providence through which it acts; therefore the smallest act of one chosen for this highest charge may be of greatest importance. Thus these ill-reputed gentle-folk endeavored to prepare and qualify for this great aim and purpose by the highest moral standards. They welcomed this misinterpretation of their belief as an opportunity for bringing a sacrifice for their high aspirations, and indeed did so on the altar of their creed.

Do not be ashamed of this happy faith of your great ancestors. Say with pride that you feel the germ of this eternal life in you. He who wishes to deprive you of this faith which forms my firm conviction, would rob you of your greatest treasure. He is certainly not your friend. He is not the man who would dare fix his gaze on a future existence. It would mean that he would have to spend his life earnestly on improvement and repentance. But this inclination to good is lacking with most men, and they find it easier to throw a veil over their past and their future.

Sholom Aleichem

Sholom Aleichem (1859 – 1916), the pen name of Solomon Rabinowitz, requires no introduction to readers of Yiddish, or any of the many languages into which his works have been translated. What is not widely known is the fact that Sholom Aleichem spent his last years in New York, where he died in 1916, mourned by 150,000 people, young and old, who lined the streets at his funeral. His will was read into the Congressional Record, and published in the New York Times, *which called it one of the great ethical wills in history.*

To be opened and published on the day of my death:

New York, 11 Tishre, 5675 (Sept. 19, 1915)

Today a great misfortune has befallen my family: my elder son, Misha (Michael Rabinowitz) has died and taken with him into the grave a part of my own life. It remains for me now to redraw my will ... which consists of ten points:

1. Wherever I may die, let me be buried not among the rich and famous, but among plain Jewish people, the workers, the common folk, so that my tombstone may honor the simple graves around me, and the simple graves honor mine, even as the plain people honored their folk writer in his lifetime.

2. No titles or eulogies are to be engraved on my tombstone, except the name Sholom Aleichem on one side and the Yiddish inscription, herein enclosed, on the other.

3. Let there be no arguments or debates among my colleagues who may wish to memorialize me by erecting a monument in New York. I shall not be able to rest peacefully in my grave if my friends engage in such nonsense. The best monument for me will be if my books are read, and if there should be among our affluent people a patron of literature who will publish and distribute my works in Yiddish or in other languages, thus enabling the public to read me and my family to live in dignity. If I haven't earned this in my lifetime, perhaps I may earn it after my death. I depart from the world with complete confidence that the public will not abandon my orphans.

4. At my grave, and throughout the whole year, and then every year on the anniversary of my death, my remaining son and my sons-in-law, if they are so inclined, should say *kaddish* for me. And if they do not wish to do this, or if it is against their religious convictions, they may fulfill their obligation to me by assembling together with my daughters and grandchildren and good friends to read this testament, and also to select one of my stories, one of the really merry ones, and read it aloud in whatever language they understand best, and let my name rather be remembered by them with laughter than not at all.

5. My children and children's children can have whatever beliefs or convictions they will. But I beg of them to guard their Jewish heritage. If any of them reject their origins to join a different faith, then that is a sign they have detached themselves from my will "and they shall have no portion and inheritance among their brethren."

6. (Here Sholom Aleichem apportions the royalties from his books and plays among his family, and for his two grand-daughters' marriage dowry).

7. From the incomes mentioned in the above paragraph, a sum shall be set aside for a foundation for Jewish authors (writing in Yiddish and Hebrew) of: 5% up to 5000 rubles a year; 10% if more than 5000 rubles. Should such a foundation exist at that time in the United States or in Europe, let this contribution be given annually to it. . . . But if such a foundation should not exist, or if one should be established that would not meet my wishes as set forth in this paragraph, then the money shall be distributed to needy writers by my heirs directly, as they may agree among themselves.

8. (He speaks here of a stone to be placed over Misha's grave in Copenhagen, where he died, *kaddish* said for him, and money given to the poor).

9. (He asks that his works be not sold in perpetuity and arranges for his family to have a permanent income from them).

10. My last wish for my successors and my prayer to my children: Take good care of your mother, beautify her old age, sweeten her bitter life, heal her broken heart; do not weep for me—on the contrary, remember me with joy; and the main thing—live together in peace, bear no hatred for each other, help one another in bad times, think on occasion of other

members of the family, pity the poor, and when circumstances permit, pay my debts, if there be any. Children, bear with honor my hard-earned Jewish name and may God in Heaven sustain you ever. Amen.

Sholom Ben Menahem Nahum Rabinowitz,
Sholom Aleichem

Appended to the will is his Epitaph, written by him in Yiddish, like the text of the will, and engraved on his tombstone in the Workmen's Circle plot in Mt. Carmel Cemetery in Brooklyn, New York:

Here lies a plain and simple Jew
Who wrote in plain and simple prose;
Wrote humor for the common folk
To help them to forget their woes.

He scoffed at life and mocked the world,
At all its foibles he poked fun,
The world went on its merry way,
And left him stricken and undone.

And while his grateful readers laughed,
Forgetting troubles of their own,
Midst their applause—God only knows—
He wept in secret and alone.

Ithamar Feinstein

Ithamar Feinstein, a Yiddish journalist early in his career, was an ardent Zionist throughout his life. His certainty about the establishment of a Jewish State "... even in our own time" seems prophetic. He attended the first Zionist Congress in Basle in 1897, and knew Theodor Herzl personally. It is further interesting to note that Ithamar Feinstein's year of birth, 1860, is the same as Herzl's. His Yiddish will was translated by his eldest son, mentioned in the will.

"And God saw everything He had created, and behold it was very good (even death).

11th February 1927
Philadelphia, Pa.

Dear Children:

I have lived through a great deal since the day when I left my birthplace in Russia. I lived through good times and times that were not so good; met all types of people, people of all shades of opinion and ideas, ideas through which a young man can be led from the proper path of life. I fought against all which was improper and sinful, and thank God, I was able to overcome them. My heart was always the most powerful stronghold to remain a *pintele yid* (a Jew to the very minutest detail), which was more to me than my very life, and of which fact I was never ashamed, no matter where I found myself. In fact I always prided myself in my Jewishness everywhere, in the circles with which I came in contact. I wish therefore to speak a few earnest words with you. I do not want to preach to you in regard to religion or belief, because this belongs to the heart of a person and we cannot force faith upon anyone. I only ask of you that, as you carry on throughout your lives, you remain loyal to your race, just as is expressed in the old and well-known Jewish saying "Vos mir zeinen, zeinen mir, ober Yidden bleiben mir" ["Whatever we are, we are; but Jews we remain"]. See to it that your children are given a Jewish training, and brought up as Jews, in the same spirit in which I raised you. Along these lines I wish to ask the help of my sons-in-law, as an act of kindness to me, and as a token of respect to me, that you do not permit your children to assimilate; above all, do not permit your children to marry those of another faith. Be proud of your Jewish ancestry, which is the pride and bulwark of all civilization. Work for the cause of Palestine (*Zion*) in every way possible, for it is the Home of our life. The hope for a Jewish Homeland in Eretz Yisrael will surely come to pass, even in our own time. Amen.

And now, my dear children, being a believer in perfect and undying faith in the survival of the soul, I wish to give you my opinion of death. When one dies, he is not actually dead, as the common understanding of the word would have it. No, as I understand it, death is only a transition from a false earthly life, a valley of sorrow, to an everlasting life, a life of truth and pleasantness. Therefore do not weep for me too much. Do not make any eulogies after my passing. Do not engrave any titles on my tombstone, excepting the following: "Here lies buried a lover of Zion, Ithamar ben Judah Feinstein, born in the month of Ab 1860. Died. . . ." I request that kaddish be recited only when you find it convenient. See to it that you sweeten your mother's bitter widowhood. I beg of you not to name any child for me unless it is certain that he will carry my proper name, Ithamar. This will should be translated into English, and I ask that my youngest son, Louis Judah, type copies of the translation and give a copy to each of his sisters. But the original will shall remain in the possession of my eldest son, Isaac Elchanan.

I leave with you my fatherly blessing, and with this, finish my will and with my own hand affix my signature.

Dora Chazin

When Dora Chazin was forty-two, desperately ill, and fearing imminent death, she wrote seven letters in rhymed Yiddish poetry, one to each of her six children and to her husband Cantor Hirsch L. Chazin, with instructions that the letters were not to be opened until her death. Happily, she recovered and lived for twenty-five more years. On the last day of shivah *the letters were read. The following letter was written to her youngest son, Pinchos, then age eight, now an eminent rabbi.*

A Letter from Dora Chazin to Her Young Son

February 11, 1923

My little son, my precious Pinchos,
Your loving mother feels she wants to say
Something to you in verse
To carry deep within your heart, forever.

Beloved child, I see before me now
The seriousness of my state;
Still, I do not question the Almighty. . . .

You are too little now to understand my writing
Nor will you much remember of
The mother's love I've given you.

I beseech God with tearful plea
To grant me yet the privilege
Of beholding with my eyes your becoming
A man excelling in all worthy things. . . .

When you become Bar Mitzvah, please Almighty God,
I hope that nothing will deter you, ever,
From *davening* the daily round of prayer
As I, your loving mother, am asking you to do.

For if, my child, you will it,
You'll find the time for it,
By developing a proper pattern
Of lying down to sleep on time,
And waking up at measured hours.

When one is good *and* keeps the rituals, my child,
Then is one beloved by everyone and everywhere.

My blessings I bestow upon you now
> For one hundred twenty years of life and great
> > fulfillment; and
> May it be true of you (and I have thought about
> > this, O so long):
> "Find favor in the eyes of God and man," in joy
> > and full contentment.

With these lines I take my leave of you;
With anguish pressing on my heart
I penned these lines, beloved child,
To be for you a remembrance everlasting.

> Your mother,
> Dora Chazin

Hayim Greenberg

Hayim Greenberg (1889 – 1953) was born in Bessarabia. In his youth he moved to Odessa and came into contact with Hayim Nahman Bialik and Menahem Mendel Ussishkin, the moving forces of the revival of Hebrew letters and culture. Hayim Greenberg emerged as a leading Zionist orator and as a writer on Jewish themes as well as on world literature and philosophy. From 1924 to the end of this life he lived in the United States. He was editor of the journal Farn Folk *until 1934, then of the Labor Zionist monthly the* Jewish Frontier.

Written in New York, April 18, 1949

The monument on my grave shall be plain, of utmost simplicity, and not a thing should be inscribed on it besides this: "Here lies Hayim Greenberg (day, month, and year)." Do not note the date of my birth: for various reasons my documents were altered several times ... and I myself do not know the precise date.

I hope that there will be no speeches at my funeral. A religious-poetic service will be sufficient. One or two psalms can be read or sung (Psalms 103, 23, 42), a chapter from Job (28)—in the original, in Yiddish, or in English—and if a suitable singer can be found, a song by Lermontov, dear to my wife and me since childhood, could be sung: "*Vichozhu odin ya na dorogu. . . .*"["I Go Out Alone Upon the Road . . ."]. If the facilities available do not prevent it, the well-known March by Chopin could be played at the end.

There are a number of men and women who brought their spiritual illumination into my own life. I hereby send to each and every one of them my profound blessing. Doubtless, there are also men and women whom I have offended and caused anguish. Of them I ask forgiveness. I erred not out of love of sin; I am guilty out of human weakness and caused hurt without any intention of hurting.

Rafael L. Savitzky

On business stationery, in beautiful Yiddish script, Rafael Savitsky of New York detailed for his children a series of vital instructions: the purpose of a tzava'ah, admonition on specific values of Judaism, burial instructions, and a detailed list of obligations and pledges to be paid. Thus his will contains all the elements of a traditional Jewish ethical will.

My beloved and devoted children, both males and females:

Inasmuch as I am not well and God alone knows whether I will ever arise from my sickbed, and who knows whether we will be able to talk during the final moments; and since it is a *mitzvah* to instruct children before death, as it is related in the holy Torah, that God says [Gen. 18:19], "For I have known him, to the end that he may command his children and his household after him, that they may keep the way of the Lord. . . ." And we find concerning King David, of blessed memory [1 Kings 2:2 – 3], "And he charged Solomon his son saying: 'I go the way of all the earth; be thou strong therefore, and show thyself a man; and keep the charge of the Lord thy God, to walk in His ways, to keep His statutes, and His commandments, and His ordinances and His testimonies, according to that which is written in the law of Moses, that thou mayest prosper in all that thou doest, and whithersoever thou turnest thyself.'" I had written many things, many points, in a previous will, the things a father says to his children; but the times have changed. Mama, of blessed memory, passed away; part of my own self also died with her. And you, my children, also went through a great deal. One who has no faith in God is not aided by that fact.

Therefore, my children, I come now to add to my testament that under all circumstances and at all times you must have trust in God. Only by having faith in God will you be able to overcome everything in the future. Children, now your true friends will be of help to you; having no mother, no father, you must always remain united; in the words of King David, "How good and how pleasant it is for brethren to dwell together in unity." In joy and in sorrow alike, brothers and sisters should stay close together—in word and deed, with a loan, with comfort and advice. You must know: "Have we not one father? Did not one God create us?" I hope that as I have been a good father to you during my lifetime, so shall I intercede in your behalf in every way.

Further, when Mama, of blessed memory, died, the Burial Society promised that I would be interred next to her, and they opened the grave lower down. I therefore request that no change be made and that our Bet Aaron Burial Society will carry this out in detail. Two weeks ago when they were here I spoke with Yudel Cohen, David Shapiro, Lezer Sosner, and Gershon Lezer Zareike. So I asked them and they promised me because they remembered what we had talked about.

Further, my daughters, remember that in America the women are the saintly souls. They hold the keys to the hearts of the men. They are the keys to the children, the keys of kashrut. Therefore, beloved daughters of mine, observe Judaism, your kosher homes, and the upbringing of the children in God's ways and in respectable ways. Then it will be well with you now and in the time to come.

Following are my obligations:

Rabbi Mareminsk	$100.00
Yaffe	300.00
Gershon (or Gershman)	200.00
Biber	50.00
Yeshivas Tiferes Yerushalayim, contribution	50.00
Chevra Tzemach Tzedek	50.00
Rifas (?)	18.00
Plumber	17.00
Meir Yona	13.00
Yerme Lavin	14.00
Meir Bloom	17.00
Chevra Bnei Aharon	15.00
Poilishe Folk Division	80.00
Yitzhok Elchonon	25.00
Torah Voda'as	25.00
Hayyim Berlin	25.00

If you fulfill my requests, God will fulfill your requests; I, your father, who writes this in full awareness and with clear mind.

Rafael L. Savitzky
[signature in Hebrew]

Monday, the week of Toldos, Heshvan 29, 5692
November 9 (in the general calendar), 1931

Samuel Lipsitz

The following will of a New England businessman, handwritten on sheets of business stationery, is remarkable for its clarity and insight. It is the more noteworthy because its author points the finger of reproof at himself for possible annoyances under the pressures of daily work alongside members of his family.

October 16, 1950
January 2, 1951

Dear Children:

Somewhere among these papers is a will made out by a lawyer. Its purpose *is to dispose of any material* things which I may possess at the time of my departure from this world to the unknown adventure beyond.

I hope its terms will cause no ill will among you. It seemed sensible when I made it. After all, it refers only to material things which we enjoy only temporarily.

I am more concerned with having you inherit something that is vastly more important.

There must be a purpose in the creation of man. Because I believe that (as I hope you will some day, for without it life becomes meaningless), I hope you will live right.

Live together in harmony! Carry no ill will toward each other. Bethink of the family. Help each other in case of need. Honor and care for your mother. Make her old age happy, as far as in your power. She deserves these things from you. It was your mother who always reproached me that I was not concerned enough about my children. She always insisted that we give them more. She would never visit a grandchild without a gift. I often felt she was too devoted a mother. Prove she was wise by being worthy of her devotion.

Carry your Jewish heritage with dignity. Though you may discard trivial ritual things, never discard your basic Jewish faith. You cannot live out your years happily without it.

Coming to the synagogue for kaddish will reacquaint you with the old prayers and you may find comfort in them as I did when your grandfather died in 1923. I was then thirty-two years old.

Being together daily in business has its disadvantage as far as a father wanting to be noble in the eyes of his children. The aggravations and the heavy pressure in our business cause friction and annoyance with one another. Maybe we said things at such times that in calm retrospect we are sorry for. I was as guilty of these things as anyone. I hope such things will not stand out in your memory of me. I must have done some worthwhile things that left good impressions and nice thoughts with you. Please recall these, or anything you feel worth carrying on, on the occasion of my *yahrzeit*. I leave with happy thoughts, because as your mother and I often said, "God has been good to us. Our children are all good, and married to good mates. Their lives can go on without us just as well. They will meet none who can speak ill of their parents."

I have enjoyed a loving and appreciative wife. She always praised and told me how capable I was. Then I had to live up to her expectations. Any worthwhile thing I ever did was due to her urging and her faith in me.

So don't mourn for me. I have enjoyed my life. Carry on from here, using the many blessing which you have (and I didn't have at your age) with wisdom and consecration to your family and mankind.

You can serve your family best by serving mankind also.

Remember me affectionately as your father.

Shmuel ben Shalom
[Signature in Hebrew]

Four Wills from One Family

The four wills that follow represent a unique phenomenon in that they were all written by members of three generations of the same family. We note the repetition of a meaningful maxim, as each of three generations sees in it a useful guidepost, takes it to its own heart, and passes it on, enhanced, to the next generation. The chain of tradition thus forged by a single family over a period of more than a hundred years speaks of a continuity much to be cherished in these times of ephemeral goals and expedient loyalties.

Benedict Blumenthal arrived in the United States in the 1850s from Germany. He settled first in Muscatine, Iowa. Later he moved to New York where B. Blumenthal and Sons became the leading producer and marketer of buttons in the United States.

My dear children, all:

With sadness I see the hour approaching when I must take my departure from you, my beloved children. The time is not far distant; all signs point that way; and I know no greater pleasure than to converse with you as my end is approaching.

To begin with, I express my hearty thanks for the love and the affection which you have bestowed on me. But I believe I have not acted differently toward you. My entire desire and strife has been to bring up good, honest children.

God has fulfilled my wish, for which I have given thanks to Him a thousand times. Let that also be your object with your descendants so that as the growing tree stands by the side of the brook, no leaf will fall off too soon, and our good name will for all times have root.

My dear children, all the wealth on earth does not equal a good name. Be kind to everybody. Do charity toward all, especially to members of the family. Had it been in my power, I would have liked to make them all rich. I started a charity fund so that my grandchildren, great-grandchildren, and those that follow should not be called upon. On the other hand, I ask you, my children, that all of you keep up this fund, so that if any of you should be in want, he will be provided for and will not need to appeal to strangers. My innermost soul tells me that that will not be necessary with you or your children. And after that it would be well to consider the next nearest relatives.

In our family, love and peace have reigned and I pray same will continue. I do not know of a more consoling thought.

I stand at the brink of the grave. I am not afraid of death and look forward to same without fear, as to die is not the worst that can befall one.

But above all, I expect from you that you will look after your dear mother in a way all children owe and should act toward their mother. She was everything to me. I would have gone long ago had it not been for her kind nursing and loving treatment. With the aid of God she lengthened my life, and had it been in her power she would have kept me much longer; but everything has its limit.

My two most favorite sayings in life were:

A heart which bothers itself with sorrow—

and the other,

A handful of earth with just a little moss.

Remember these. There is much sense and a lot of good teaching in them.

Take care that your descendants get a good education. Don't mind the cost, because education is the safest investment. The main thing you want to instill in your children is Truthfulness. The best pillow is a clear conscience.

Almighty God in Heaven, I pray to You that such a pillow be the lot of my children and that they will rest peacefully thereon till their worldly trip is ended and their spirit passes to the Almighty God. This is the last wish of your father who loves you to the last minute.

Following the death of Benedict Blumenthal, his grandson, Gustav, succeeded him as leader of the firm. The following testament was written by Gustav Blumenthal in 1924.

November, 1924

My dear Beloved Ones:

It is a bright sunshiny day. I am feeling well and happy and yet I realize that the inevitable may come at any moment, perhaps soon and possibly only in distant years.

When it does, I feel that you would give most anything to be able to have just one additional moment to tell me of the love you have for me, even so I imagine those expressions of love and affection which I will never hear and answer them now, by telling you that I fully realized while among you that the family tie between us could not have been more sweet, sincere, and helpful, and my hope is that whatever may arise in the future, the same conditions may exist between you and yours.

I enclose translation of a letter written by my father's father (original in my box at home). Men's hearts and innermost sentiments were no different then than they are now, nor than they will be in generations to come.

If you consider it appropriate, have this translation of my grand-father's letter read at my funeral services; it expresses my thoughts and sentiments as well as if I had written them myself.

And so perhaps amid the first pangs of sorrow, these farewell words of mine may help to cheer you and animate each one of you to do noble deeds and lead a helpful life.

Continue to be honest, charitable men and women and instill in the hearts of your children and those that follow that "A clear conscience *is* the best pillow."

A farewell embrace for each of you. Keep on loving me in memory as I loved you in life.

Father

Gustav's son Robert, a graduate of Andover and Yale, joined the firm and in turn became its president. His will below was written in 1927 and he died several years later, in his early thirties.

February 10, 1927

My dear ones:

As I at best am only a poor imitation of *my* dear father, I must once again follow his lead. It is my wish, as it was his, that the letter of my father to us and that of his grandfather to his children be read at my funeral. If I have no children, the passages should be changed so as to be appropriate and so as to refer to Dotty and Julian Jr. and Doris instead of mother and us.

You all know that you had all my love—my darling wife, my sweet mother, my dear sister and her children. Keep fresh and constantly in your minds the thoughts, sayings, and ideals of my father—he was so far and away the most marvelous and wonderful man of us all.

A clear conscience *is* the best pillow.

Keep on loving me in memory as I loved you in life.

Bobbie

The writer of this will, Carrie Blumenthal, was the widow of Gustav and the mother of Robert. It was written in 1956, two years before her death.

May 29, 1956

My dear children:

If I were to write you a farewell letter telling of my love and devotion for you all, I could do no better than to reiterate the statements and sentiments of your dear father, grandfather, and great-grandfather written three years before he died, February 7, 1927. As I have now reached the ripe age of eighty-seven and am living on borrowed time, I would like to express a word as regards my funeral. Choose the most convenient place for yourselves. *If you see fit,* I should like to have the letter of my husbands' grandfather read at my funeral. It was read at both my husband's and dear Bobbie's funerals. It would please me if my grandson Julian Bach, who has such a gift for speaking, would read the letter, so full of love and sentiment for his children.

Thank you all again for your love and devotion, and [I] hope I have not caused you any trouble or anxiety. A farewell embrace to you all. Keep on loving me in memory, as you loved me in life.

Fondly your devoted mother, grandmother, and great-grandmother

Allen Hofrichter

On a day between Yom Kippur 1973 and August 21, 1974, the day of his death, Allen Hofrichter wrote the following will. In the brief space of less than two typewritten pages he says much and implies even more about himself, his beliefs and expectations. He is a realist about the world, but does not rail against it as, in recognizing human imperfection, he observes, "Gratitude is the Mayfly of all virtues . . . life if too crowded to observe the ordinary amenities."

I have requested my children not to engage the services of a rabbi. He never knew me and his eulogy cannot be anything but erratic and traditionally fulsome. Nor in his peroration will the few interlarded Hebrew phrases that few can understand be an "open sesame" to heaven.

Credit Sybil and me with this one indisputable fact: that no one, from Sybil's family or mine, has ever been turned away when they came to us for assistance. When we had no funds, we even pawned our insurance; but in no case has anyone had his request denied. The pity of it is that no one of the score or more we have helped has been interested enough to inquire how Sybil and I are faring.

Nor do I fault them for this. Gratitude is the Mayfly of all virtues, and in this hectic world, life is too crowded to observe the ordinary amenities.

We have adhered to the biblical injunction, and in our contributions to others we have more than tithed ourselves.

After the Yom Kippur War we received a warm and most gratifying letter from Hadassah of which the following is a quote:

> You will be interested to know that the wing at the Hadassah Hospital that bears your name was the most crowded with wounded soldiers almost shattered by the fighting in this recent war. The orthopedic surgeons were operating around the clock, and after the recovery room, the patients were then sent to the Orthopedic section—The Hofrichter Wing.

I have tried to be a good father. How successful I have been, only my two children know. But this I am sure they must realize, that no sacrifice on my part was too great, no amount of thought and effort was too much for me to assure their comfort, peace, and happiness.

They repaid me generously. Our grandchildren, Richard and Michael, and those blessed chattering angels whom I adore, Lisa, Sharon, and Evie, have brightened my declining years.

What can I say about Sybil, my wife these many years. Sybil of the low, gentle voice, the ready laugh, and the soft, ministering hands. For forty-odd years we can honestly say that we have never gone to bed angry with each other. Not a day ever passed without an overt attempt to show our affection for each other; whatever our moods, we were as one.

She extolled my triumphs, belittled my failures, and in her eyes I possessed all virtues and no faults. She was the better part of me, a gentler, more forgiving part.

When our family was younger and we lived in Suffern and Sybil lit the candles ushering in the Sabbath, the world outside our door was nonexistent, an ineffable peace entered our house, and Sybil's presence filled the room like a benediction on all of us.

Her handicap? She disavowed it and laughed more in one day than most women laugh in a month. We were as one. Nothing could come between us to mar our joy in each other.

By this time I am sure Sybil's nose is pink and her eyes are welling with tears. Don't cry, Sybil. I'm at peace at last. No aches, no pains, and happily, no doctors or hospitals. You've given me a good life, and I am grateful. I hope there is a heaven and that I will be admitted there so that I may continue to love you as I have on earth.

To my children, I need not foreswear you to love and cherish your mother, to guard and protect and shield her from any hurts this ugly world may direct at her. Be good to her. She amply deserves your devotion, and please, please do not let her feel alone and lonely.

To all who are here, be well and stay well and may your remaining years be as full of happiness, joy, and peace as mine have been.

Bless you all.

Jennie Stein Berman

Jennie Berman was brought to America from Lithuania by her family, which settled in Ohio. Following her marriage she lived in Chicago until the end of her life. Her children and grandchildren remember her as fully observant of Jewish tradition, but very progressive and modern in outlook. A granddaughter recalls her "dressing like a princess for the Sabbath." Sam, for whom she is concerned, is a bachelor brother. The date of this letter is 1956.

To all my children:

This is your mother's last wish. After I am gone, you should always be together and well and happy; and of what is left in money I want you to *share* and *share alike*. Florence, Alvin, Julius, Lester, if it is only one dollar you should each get a fourth of it. That is my last wish. And if I go before Sam, you should all see to it that he has a place to sleep with something to eat at all times. Please. Then I can rest in peace. That is my last wish, that you all be well and happy. And I give you all my

Blessing and Love
Mother
This is my last wish.

Leonard Ratner

The following note was found among the papers of Leonard Ratner following his death in the mid-1970s. An immigrant to the United States, the writer attained exceptional success and was a noted philanthropist. He expresses his desire that his children and grandchildren emulate the charitable deeds of his deceased wife, their mother and grandmother.

To my Family . . . and Grandchildren

This is my last letter and when you will read it, I will only be memory.

I don't think that I have to write you much as, thank God, you are educated and smart enough to understand that this world is not easy. I am sure you will endure it and will continue to follow in the footsteps of mother, as she was one of the greatest women who ever lived.

The luckiest thing for me was meeting your mother, and she to some extent was responsible for many of the successes in our life as she was not only looking for herself but what can be done for the family and others. To some extent she copied our grandparents. I am sure you will continue the kind of life and keep close with all our families and try to do as much as you can for each other.

Don't forget your seats at the Park Synagogue.

Stay well and keep up your good work.

Your Father, Grandfather

✠ *Harold*

I address myself to my children—to all of our household. My father died at the age of 83 and I have a premonition that in this, my 83rd year, I too will be called to my final resting place. . . .

My deep concern is for your mother. What will become of her if I should be the first? She is so dependent on me. I pray to God and ask Him to prolong her sister's life so that they may spend the rest of their lives together. By that I mean that Fanny should move in with Mom.

. . . All my life I have tried to help others without expecting anything in return—and now I make a simple request—call Mom if possible every day—visit her once a week—dine with her once a week—call her and tell her what you want for dinner—make her laugh, have the children call, and visit her once in a while. When she is away, write to her frequently. Do it not as an obligation but because I know you really love her and want to make her happy.

Forgive me if I hurt you by suggesting this—I mean well—I am very proud of you and love you all dearly. I am grateful for the many blessings He has showered upon us one and all. In fact I feel that we have received more than our share of *naches* [parental pleasure].

And now I must make a confession. For the past few months I have gradually developed a hate for money and what it does to people. I honestly feel that if one reaches the stage where he has provided fully for his family and himself, the balance does not belong to him. It is a lend-lease from the Almighty to distribute to charity. If I survive I will try to spend the rest of my life seeking out avenues of worthwhile charities, preferably in Israel.

Mother and I lived modestly. I never succeeded in convincing her to buy a mink coat. She always felt that was showing off. I lived the same way. If we lived luxuriously we could never have helped the families for most of our married life.

You have now reached the stage where you can broaden your philanthropy and in larger amounts. I hope and pray that my and your children will follow the same pattern. The children should have begun long ago. Teach them to put aside from their allowance and from any money they earn for charity. Do it now.

Above all—be forever vigilant for those in need and don't wait until they ask you—that is humiliating.

One last request—when the time comes for my last journey, I would like Mother's and my casket facing each other—she on my right side—all it needs is to place the caskets at an angle, like this:

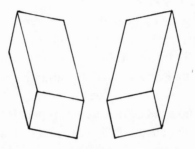

Fare Well

A Woman Writes to Her Husband and Children

Long ago many Jews believed to speak of death was to invite the Angel of Death to visit. This then is not a statement of death but a legacy to Life.

The thoughts in my mind today, 5 Tishre 5740 — September 25, 1979, will be as true and complete at any time that you may read them. They are the expressions of my love and hopes for you, my beloved husband, and dear children.

To my husband: We have had a life closely woven together by our work and leisure. You have always been my closest and best friend. It's more difficult to be the one who survives because you must face the worldly aches and pains—but now alone.

Please remarry a woman who will share life's burdens and joys with you, rather than just the marriage bed. Although our children are always there in the pinch, you need a life independent of theirs; so choose a mate wisely and with my blessing.

To David, my first born: I hope to know the day when you find your way. You have the one basic ingredient that will make you a success in life—your honesty. Believe in yourself, as I believe in you, establish your goals, work hard toward them, and you will succeed.

Someday I hope you will embrace Judaism as part of your life. It's never too late to come back to your faith—once a Jew always a Jew.

To Risa, my only daughter: I swell with pride when I see how much in control you are of your life. Please use your mind and body wisely. When you marry, I hope you will keep the Jewish faith. A solid marriage is a difficult task. A strong foundation and similar religious and economic background are like cement in keeping a marriage together. You know you have the power to do anything you choose, so use this power wisely.

Jamie, my good-natured son—who can never remain mad or hold

a grudge. You have been blessed with special talents. Fulfill your potential by seeking lofty goals; and when you are successful, remember to think of the less fortunate and find a meaningful way to contribute to society. Talent is God-given and you can repay your Maker by giving in return.

To you all—I'm glad you're my family; I'll always be with you and you with me in one way or another.

Love,

Mom

Rosie Rosenzweig

The number of ethical wills written by women in the modern period is far greater than by women in earlier periods. This is in keeping with other, ongoing, salutary social developments. What is equally noteworthy is the observation that in their ethical wills women more often than men draw upon psychological insights to personalize their hopes and counsel. Rosie Rosenzweig is a contemporary wife and mother residing on the East coast. In addressing her children she individualizes her hopes for them on the basis of strengths and inclinations they possess. This emphasis, whether conscious or unconscious on the part of the writer, is reminiscent of the mode of the patriarchal blessings in Genesis 49 and in Deuteronomy 33.

This will, and the one that follows, was written at a workshop on ethical wills that was conducted at her synagogue Beth El of Sudbury, Massachusetts, as a way of preparing for Yom Kippur.

7/25/79
5 Tishre 5740

My dear family:

It seems appropriate that I just mailed a proof of a correction on my father's tombstone to the monument people. I was concerned . . . with the correct manner of recording his good name. He was a *Kohen,* of the priestly class, and it had to be so recorded.

So is my link to you, not of words on dead stone, nor nitpicking, but of the good way to keep a good name, as a member of the family you came from, the family you'll spawn and the tribe from whose roots you flower.

Shakespeare did say "A rose by any other name still smells as sweet" (I know I had to remember that during my days on the printing press), but so it is with character from which emanates the good name . . . you can be in rags, in a poor state, a misunderstood laborer, a misunderstood professional . . . but your good character will earn you your way. It goes without saying you'll work hard toward your chosen goal by education, by working at occupations up the ladder, etc., but it is the uses of your intelligence as you would use it to build character that I would address now.

If there is a pleasure in acquiring knowledge, there is greater pleasure in applying it.

But what knowledge is useful to the end of building character?

I wish for you the joys of understanding the knowledge of our tradition to its deepest soul. I guarantee it will resonate in your heart at times of deepest trouble and soundest joy. There is a mellowness I would wish for you in your later years, that I now am just beginning to perceive.

For instance, take the commandment "Thou shalt have no other Gods before you." If the name of God, "Yehovah," means the future tense of "to be," then you as His reflection should also always be becoming . . . working for a future image of yourself, a better self of more enduring character. You take *teshuvah* [repentence] seriously, you change, you redeem your life, you take Yom Kippur seriously . . . and when you do this which is your tradition and your best selves, I live for you, my living heritage, my ever-bearing fruits.

I urge you to understand your roots, as they are in you as archetypes and beg you not to deny [them]. The Torah teaches logic, values, and history. For example, if you pass your enemy in trouble you are bidden to help him as you can and go on your way. Logically the seeds of a better future are here. Rabbi Jacob is quoted in *Sayings of the Fathers* (4:21) that this life is like a waiting room before the bigger banquet. Logically one should always be in preparation. This not only refers to afterlife but to your passages in life from decade to decade.

So many words I've written and so many generalizations. What about specifics:

I would like you to know my writings and keep them . . . however little of significance or insignificance I've produced. I want my grandchildren to know the fancies of my mind. That is who I am and all of substance I can give them. I leave three notebooks full of experiences with the weekly Torah Service. If nothing else, pass these on. This is my most important life through the decades. Keep family records, of our history, our events. It is a pleasure I want you to have. The only stability in a drifting society is the fabric of our family. Know who are its members and of what character.

It would be nice to always keep the house in some form.

Elizabeth, I wish for your happiness and stability. That your feelings fly toward the dream of fulfillment but still be balanced by your keen intelligence, is what I hope for you. I hope you remember our times of understanding, and wherever I am I will send whatever healing is possible. I trust the mountain-guide sense in you to go to peaks I'll never see. Be there for me.

Benjamin, I wish that your keen intellectual nature be rounded by that intuition that comes from the artist in you. At thirteen your insight into the *Akedah* was remarkable. May that become more cultivated as you grow older. I live for you in the applause of that day, that brightened your face, and the applause now for such continued adventurous and original trailblazing.

Rachel, my youngest, who has my name and my old place in the family, the youngest, I want to leave you only my best qualities and not my worst. Listen to the still, small voice of the best in yourself, regardless of what the people around you feel. Be swayed only by wisdom, and not the momentary emotions of others.

Sandy, should you outlive me, I release you to the memories of those happinesses that endured and survive me. I know you will forget all else. I urge you to hold on to your visions but ground them in reality. We will meet again as no quantum in the universe dies but is attracted to others for whom it has charge. If I have outlived you I go to meet you now.

Remember, please, to talk to one another on the anniversary of my death, and forgive me for my transgressions against you. Of all other dealings, the commonsense *mitzvot*, the good values, the way to deal with people and each other, I need leave you no further instructions. You have been rigorously schooled by me, and I assume you will know how to put my body to rest. . . .

Live out your lives wisely, well, and with few regrets.

Your loving mother

William Joseph Adelson

William Joseph Adelson, a contemporary father and husband, was a member of that same study group at Congregation Beth El of Sudbury, Massachusetts, that prepared for Yom Kippur by writing ethical wills. He is a pediatrician and an allergist whose interests include painting, sculpture, and photography. He and his wife are the craftsmen who made the Eternal Light in their synagogue.

5 Tishre 5740

My Dearest Family:

In the busy and often structured pace of our lives there have rarely been times to stand back and reflect upon the big and important things. Our attention has usually been taken by practical details. I want to tell you about what I consider really important.

I was fortunate in time and place. I was born in the America of challenge and opportunity because my parents succeeded in the struggle to get here. I was spared the danger and tragedy of pogroms, of the Holocaust, of major war, of starvation and human misery. I was free to strive and to achieve—to set my goals high and to realize their fruition.

I have always been an optimist. I have never really regretted any of the choices I have made—although I could have lived and been happy with other choices.

I have been blessed with a happy and understanding first marriage and with a happy and sharing second one. I cannot leave you the example of lifelong steadfastness. Let me instead leave you the example of compassion and flexibility. When an old relationship became lost, both your mother and I were honest and insightful enough to recognize this—to make the break, releasing one another and leaving one another free to find new happiness.

Life is imperfect—yet in its living lies ever-renewed excitement.

I have been privileged to watch each of you grow up and move out into the world. I have enjoyed watching your interests and skills develop. I have offered you what I had to share, but have not been disappointed when you have each said, "No thanks—I will find my own thing and do it." I have been pleased that each of you has taken pride in doing what you do well. Quality has its own rewards. Yet flexibility is also important. It is important to be able to let something go if it doesn't prove to be as important or necessary or satisfying as you had thought. You are not enslaved by the rigidity of your aspirations.

I have enjoyed watching you share things with one another. Next to your own husbands or wives and children, the closest affinities you can have will be with one another. You know one another's weaknesses as well as strengths. You have generally supported one another. You have helped one another. I don't ever remember telling you to do that. Chalk that one up as an undeserved bonus for me.

I have felt it important to have you establish your own priorities. I have respected those priorities.

I have tried to set an example for you in active participation in the Jewish and secular communities. I have always felt the importance of sharing in these dimensions. You are young and I cannot tell whether you will be so inclined. It would please me if you found some of the same enthusiasm and excitement in the Jewish tradition that I have. (Or if not in that, I hope you will participate actively in some spiritual tradition.) It is a dimension of spirit that can bring great meaning and intensity to your lives.

I hope you will also enjoy musical, artistic, and intellectual interests. One can live without these aspects, but they enormously enhance the quality of life. I hope you will always feel close to nature—aware of the many subtleties and miracles that unfold constantly around us and in harmony with these cycles. I hope you will share some of these deep gratifications and awarenesses with your spouses and children, and that you will have the maturity to not expect them to necessarily accept your sharing or see things as you do.

I hope you will continue to have intense interests—although these may change. Disappointments may be more painful, but achievements are more gratifying.

I hope you will have compassion for your brothers and sisters—both Jews and non-Jews. That you will ever strive to help those who need the help—that you will ever speak out against injustice and bigotry—that you will never become smug and complacent because you *have* when others *have not*. All people deserve the feeling of respect and realization in their lives. I hope you can help many attain it.

To my beloved Paula—you stepped into such a big job. It has been hard for you to catch up with the complicated life of the family. You have done wonderfully in understanding my needs and pressures. It has been hard for you, coming from differing family background, to cope with assertive, grown children. You have really tried to grow and extend yourself.

You have accommodated yourself to a hard and demanding pace. I hope you will have enjoyed the race of our lives together as much as I have enjoyed sharing it with you.

When I am gone—all of the things I possess will have no further meaning to me. Although I have not left you all objects of great value, I hope you will want some of the things I have created and that we have accumulated over the years. I would be pleased to have you share these things among you—taking those that please each of you or have special meaning for you. Be magnanimous if more than one of you want a particular thing.

More than material possessions, I hope I will have left each of you:

an optimistic spirit
a fervor and enthusiasm for life
a sensitivity to nature and esthetics
a closeness and regard for one another
a sense of responsibility and concern for others
and a sense of worthwhileness about your selves.

I wish your life may be as good and satisfying as mine has been, and thank each of you for having contributed to it.

Lovingly,
Dad and Bill

Hayyim and Esther Kieval

The following selection is taken from a contemporary ethical will written by a father, in Albany, New York, in his name and in the name of his wife. It is written in the form of a letter from both parents. Rabbi Kieval is the spiritual leader of Temple Israel in Albany, New York, and the author of a commentary on the High Holiday Prayerbook. Esther, his wife, is a Seminary graduate and a community leader.

In addition to making out the usual last will and testament and the usual financial and family arrangements, it has always been a beautiful Jewish tradition to leave to one's beloved children what is called an Ethical Will or *tzava'ah*. You will remember that the first fathers of our people, Avraham, Yitzhak, and Ya'akov, gave blessings and other guidance to their children upon which they might draw when their parents were no longer with them in life. Your dear mother and I, of course, hope and pray that we shall be with you to help and guide you for many, many years; but at the same time if (God forbid) we should not be able to fulfill this deep desire, we wanted to share some thoughts with you at this time on what we consider to be the most important things in our life.

First and foremost, we want you to know that we have had a very happy life so far and that we are full of thanksgiving and gratitude to God for all our blessings. Even if (God forbid) we would have to say good-bye today, we would not feel that we have been cheated by life or forgotten by God. Life is a precious gift from a Power greater than ourselves and beyond ourselves. One must be thankful always for as much or as little as he or she receives from the Divine Source of life. It is the deepest wish of your parents that you will not only grow up to be healthy in body and mind and that you will lack nothing in the way of material needs, but that you will also continue to live according to the ideals and values which your parents have cherished all our lives and which have given us so much happiness.

It would be foolish for us to command you in these matters. You must and you will, of course, live your own lives. We only hope and pray that, as your parents and teachers, we have succeeded in filling your hearts with a love and reverence for the Torah, for the Jewish people and its religious way of life, and above all for God. God unites parents and their children even when they are far apart from one another, even when one generation is in the land of the living and the other is in the world of Eternity. The Universe is one, and in the mind of God there is no difference certainly between the living and the dead, nor can there be any difference in the care and concern which God gives to all the creatures.

Of the many blessings which Mother and I have enjoyed in our lives so far, we tend to forget the great privilege of being Americans and all the precious freedoms and opportunities that go with it. Though Mother was born in a foreign country and I in this land, we have both loved the United States equally, and tried at all times to be loyal and contributing citizens. This too we pray will be your way all your lives. It is sometimes difficult for people to see how it is possible to love America with all their heart and soul, and also to love the Jewish people and the Holy Land of our people "with all your heart and with all your soul and with all your might." But when one has enough love, one can manage to love many people and many things that deserve love, without conflict. Mother and I have never felt any such conflict and we are confident that you will also find the way to do this.

We ask you to forgive us all the angry moments we have shown you and pardon whatever pain, sadness, or shame we may ever have caused you. Let all these less-than-happy memories be illuminated by the endless and bottomless love which we have always had for you. You have given us so much joy, so much pride, so much *nachat* [parental pleasure], that I would not know how to begin to describe it. I wish I had the time and the words to write separately (for Mother and myself) to each of you, each in his or her own language according to his or her understanding. But, somehow, we hope that you will know what we are trying to say.

No matter what may happen, know and believe that Mother and Daddy will always love you, always be with you, always be united with you through God, who is the loving Father of us all. I shall end this letter to you, dear children, with all our love and kisses. Try to remember us and always love each other.

Nitzah Marsha Jospe

Some ethical wills are written in an hour or a day, others over longer periods. Some are written in prime health, others in the grip of infirmities of age or disease. Nitzah Marsha Jospe (1947 – 1980), young Denver wife and mother, felt impelled to record her thoughts and feelings during the closing months of her struggle with the ravaging illness that claimed her before her thirty-third birthday. In a magnificent eulogy, her husband incorporated selections from her notebook and diary, culminating with a letter to her children. Brief excerpts from the eulogy provide continuity and a frame for the ethical will of a remarkable, courageous woman.

---

25 Adar 5740
March 13, 1980

We all knew, as did Nitzah, that this time would come, but that knowledge could still not prepare us for the final loss. I have some thoughts I'd like to share with you, but more important, I'd like to share with you some of Nitzah's thoughts as well.

At no time did Nitzah delude herself about herself or her condition. She faced her disease realistically, and with remarkable equanimity. On the day we left Israel, the *Jerusalem Post* ran an article about a journalist we had met a few times and with whom Nitzah had discussed, with her typical frank honesty, her disease and our cancer self-help program. The article, while not mentioning Nitzah by name, mentioned a program this journalist was planning with a woman "dying of cancer." Some of our family and friends begged me to keep it from Nitzah, to spare her feelings from this rather blunt reference. But, perhaps inevitably, Nitzah saw a copy of the paper with the article on the plane back to America. When I told her of the concern of our family and friends for her feelings, she wrote down her own reaction to the article and to their desire to shield her from its brutal reference to her. She wrote:

> Your concern continues to astound me because I don't know how I deserve it, but I certainly don't want you to be overprotective. I had to laugh that anyone would think I would be upset by the *Jerusalem*

Post article. The subject is one that I talked about with her [i.e., the journalist]—it's no surprise to me that the doctors do not have a cure for my disease and consider it terminal. The whole purpose of the course Raphi and I have gone through was to deal with all possibilities, including death and dying, and this is far from the first time the subject has occurred to me or been openly discussed by me. There are lots of things I'm very emotional about, but this article was certainly not one of them. Thank you for trying to protect me, but it was totally unnecessary.

During the last few months of her life, Nitzah kept a diary, and I would like to share with you a few of her thoughts. She always offered to let me read her diary, so I don't think she would mind my reading some selections to you.

Tuesday, 8 Kislev 5740, November 27, 1979
Our session tonight was on death and dying—very appropriate for me this week and very good. It's better to think about it and sort it out than push it away. I'm even supposed to write my own obituary, and I think I can.

After we returned from Israel, where Nitzah was incredibly energetic, full of life and joy, she seemed to recognize that she would not be able to continue much longer, and her tone changed somewhat.

Saturday night, 17 Tevet 5740, January 5, 1980
For my obituary, I've always imagined age 33. It's the magic number. If I were to make it to 34, I think I could make it to 120. But somehow May seems very far away. . . . I think I have to try harder to live up to what I said when I first got sick—if this does not kill me, there is no need to let it occupy my time and thoughts; and if it does, then it shouldn't be allowed to interfere with the time that's left. I do hope it will be good time, not bad.

Her last entry starts with thoughts of our youngest, Tamar:

Sunday, Rosh Hodesh Adar 5740, February 17, 1980
She's a good girl, and is learning all kinds of English sentences, and

I've tried to spend as much time with her as she wanted. But I'm afraid she won't remember me. I'm not even sure what Ilan at 4½ will remember—not much I'm sure; and Deena at 7½ may remember some harsh things because for her it has been pretty negative lately, and I'll try to make things better when I go back, but I find I'm very tired. . . . I feel sometimes I could go on forever, and at other times that I wish the end would come. . . .

Most important, to our children: If you cannot understand me now, perhaps you will read and understand these words when you are older. Your Ima's greatest frustration was the realization that you might not remember her at all, or that you might remember her only as she was sick, and not always able to express to you properly her love for you. Your Ima wanted very much for you to know her love for you. Since she knew that she might not be able to say this to you at the end, and since you may only understand this when you are older, she wrote a letter to the three of you. This is your Ima's last letter to you, which she gave to me:

> I can't really tell you what I want for you, because even now I don't know what I want for myself. What is important is to make each day good, and not to say "tomorrow" or "in the future it will be better." Happiness is a goal, but not something we must have every moment. That is not life.
>
> I want you to be good Jews. It's something I've always been proud of. . . . I would like to be able to help you and enjoy you, just as my parents did with me. Since that is not possible, I want you to know how much I love you. I wish you had more memories of me to help you know me.
>
> Sometimes the memories are better than the reality.
>
> The saddest part is leaving you and not knowing how you will develop. I would like to think you will be good, honest people, who have enough self-esteem and self-worth to stand up for yourselves, and not be afraid to say what you think.
>
> Don't think anyone else is better than you are. You are as good as anyone. Every person is special, and so is each of you; not just to me, but to yourselves.

You, of course, want your own things from your own life, but parents can't help having dreams for their children.

You mustn't be bound by what I would like for you. I expect you to go your own way as good people, the best way you know how.

These were your Ima's parting words to you, her *tzava'ah,* her ethical will and instructions to guide you as you grow up.

William Lewis Abromowitz

New York — born William Lewis Abromowitz (1914 — 1972) was a prominent scientist and industrial leader of Swampscott, Massachusetts. He was a leader in his synagogue, in the work of Weizmann Institute, and in behalf of numerous other worthy causes. The product of a traditional Jewish family, he maintained a lifelong devotion to Jewish learning and to its advancement.

Jerusalem, 1963

Dearest Lee, Susan, Gail, Kenneth, and Ava,

Weep not and dry your tears. At least in my behalf. The years that God has allotted to me have been good, and I have no *tayneh* [complaint] to our Maker. Death is the final state of all human beings, and a few years more or less do not matter. I have drunk fully of the cup of life, and a few remaining drops left unsipped will cause me no grief or regrets. If there is one thing I ask, it is that I may be permitted to see all my children happily married; if not, I'll be watching from somewhere anyway. Marriage is the fulfillment of life, and I have been blessed with a jewel of a wife and four wonderful children whose love has sustained me during those times that try a man's soul and has nourished me during times of *simhah* [joy].

To my wife: Your love has been to me beyond measure. Remember what has been and weep not. Time is a wonderous healer even as you and I have recovered from but not forgotten the loss of our son and our parents. You are too much of a woman to live alone, and the children will mature and go their own way. Look for a man you can respect and love and know that I only want you to be happy.

To my children: In material things I have seen to it that you will not want. These are the least important things, although the lawyer has prepared a *megillah* to safeguard them. Remember to be Jews, and the rest will follow as day follows night. Our religion is not ritual but a way of life. To us as Jews, life is its own *raison d'être,* its own self-justification; we await neither heaven nor hell. Ritual is only a tool to remind us who we are and of the divine commandments. Jews do not lie, steal, nor bear false witness—*past nisht,* as our parents used to say—such things are simply unbecoming for a Jew. Take care of one another, and in honoring your mother, honor yourselves. I know the love she has lavished on you without thought of self.

Marry within your faith, not to please me, but so that you may be happy, not because gentiles are inferior—they are not—but because marriage is complex enough without the complicating variables of different viewpoints. You are the bearers of a proud tradition of four thousand years. Do not let the torch drop in your generation.

Never turn away from anyone who comes to you for help. We Jews have seen more suffering than any other people; therefore we should care more. That which you give away, whether of money or of yourselves, is your only permanent possession.

To my son: I mention you first, not because I love you more, but because you will now be the head of the family. The girls may call this sexism, but I hope they will forgive me. Don't fail your sisters or your mother. Their tears are my tears. Money is only a tool and not an end in itself. Your grandfather taught me that a man should earn his money till the age of forty, enjoy it till fifty, and then give it away, that a man who dies rich is a failure as a human being. I say this because I know that your abilities will make you a wealthy man materially. But my real desire is that you be rich in heart and soul. . . .

Don't forget Israel. You can be a builder of the homeland for the remnants of our people. There is no conflict between your obligation as a citizen of our country and your concern for Israel. On the contrary, a good Jew is a better American.

To my daughters: You are warmblooded. Jewish girls keep themselves clean, not because sex is dirty—it is not—but because the love you will bring your husbands should not be sullied by experimentation or dalliance. It has always been the Jewish mother who has preserved our people. I shall be content if you follow in the path of your mother.

To all of you: Let your word be your bond! Those mistakes that I regret most keenly are the times when I let human weakness forget this. I know it is hard to learn from the experiences of others, especially of parents, but if there is one thing I beg you to take to heart, it is this.

Say kaddish *after* me, not *for* me. Kaddish is the unique Jewish link that binds the generations of Israel. The grave doesn't hear the kaddish, *but the speaker does,* and the words will echo in your heart. The only immortality I seek is that my children and my children's children be good Jews, and thereby good people.

God bless you and keep you. I love you.

Your father

Jacob J. Weinstein

Rabbi Jacob J. Weinstein (1902–1974) was the spiritual leader of K.A.M. congregation, Kehillat Anshe Ma'arav, Chicago's oldest synagogue, from 1939 until 1967. He was an outspoken supporter of labor and an expert in matters relating to the labor movement. Rabbi Weinstein served as president of the Central Conference of American Rabbis and chairman of its Committee on Justice and Peace.

November 1971

It was a custom in ancient times for the father to leave an ethical will together with the legal testament. I hesitate to follow in this fine tradition for fear of imposing my will on yours. The state of the world which I leave you hardly testifies to the wisdom of my generation or those immediately before. I would be remiss, however, if I did not warn your generation that, in your anger and frustration, you fail to distinguish between the conventions that enshrine the past because it is the past and the traditions which have in them the seed of a more meaningful future. There is no single, simple, or automatic way in which one can learn the art of this discretion, but I sincerely believe that the history and teachings of Judaism contain implicit and explicit guidelines for achieving a viable synthesis between the tried values of the past and the liberating needs of the present and the future. This belief and the understandable, though inarticulate, loyalty to the choices of a lifetime compel me to urge you to "consider well the rock whence you were digged" [Isa. 51:1].

The attrition of the tradition in my lifetime is evident—there is a real danger that it will disappear in your children's lives. I would consider this an affront to the principle of continuity and a loss of a fine family resource. I know I cannot impose my values and judgments on you, but I can and do request that you not let this heritage go by default but that you study it, participate in it, and make your decision on the basis of knowledge as well as sentiment. You will find that it may be a very real help in holding you together as a family. One of the most painful experiences I have had as a rabbi has been to witness the weakening of family ties—brothers and sisters who come together at funerals and weddings as strangers asking querulously of each other: "Why have we not heard from you? Why do we have to wait for a funeral to bring us together?" As love becomes more ambient, less focused, more dependent on necessity and convenience, it will need the more elemental instinctive support of family affection, of common womb genesis. So hold fast to the family affection you have so far maintained and try to pass it on to your children.

Instead of any formal visiting of the grave, I would prefer that the family try to observe a family day in the month of June at which reminiscences of happy incidents be the order of the day, and some worthy cause be remembered in fulfillment of the admonition *tzedakah tatzil mimavet*—"Charity (or social justice) saves from death" [Prov. 10:2, 11:4].

Sam Levenson

Sam Levenson was raised and educated in New York. He taught in New York City high schools for fifteen years before making a successful career as a humorist. He became a beloved, nationally known personality through his books and appearances on radio and television; he had his own program, the "Sam Levenson Show," on Columbia Broadcasting System television. The major focus of his humor was the family—raising children and growing up in an urban environment. Some of his writings appear in textbooks on urban sociology. It has been said of his humor that it was of a special kind: it sought laughter at nobody's expense. This is his "Ethical Will and Testament to His Grandchildren, and to Children Everywhere."

I leave you my unpaid debts. They are my greatest assets. Everything I own—I owe:

1. To America I owe a debt for the opportunity it gave me to be free and to be me.

2. To my parents I owe America. They gave it to me and I leave it to you. Take good care of it.

3. To the biblical tradition I owe the belief that man does not live by bread alone, nor does he live alone at all. This is also the democratic tradition. Preserve it.

4. To the six million of my people and to the thirty million other humans who died because of man's inhumanity to man, I owe a vow that it must never happen again.

5. I leave you not everything I never had, but everything I had in my lifetime: a good family, respect for learning, compassion for my fellowman, and some four-letter words for all occasions: words like "help," "give," "care," "feel," and "love."

Love, my dear grandchildren, is easier to recommend than to define. I can tell you only that like those who came before you, you will surely know when love ain't; you will also know when mercy ain't and brotherhood ain't.

The millennium will come when all the "ain'ts" shall have become "ises" and all the "ises" shall be for all, even for those you don't like.

Finally, I leave you the years I should like to have lived so that I might possibly see whether *your* generation will bring more love and peace to the world than ours did. I not only hope you will. I pray that you will.

Grandpa Sam Levenson

Abraham M. Ellis

Abraham M. Ellis (1880 – 1960) was an erudite, highly respected businessman and philanthropist of Philadelphia. His lucidly written ethical will is the distillation of a thoughtful life spent in gainful, constructive enterprise and in civic service. Although European-born, he was thoroughly Americanized, a public-spirited citizen whose deepest motives flowed from the traditions of his fathers which he imbibed in his youth. His will, in the form of a book about forty pages in length, is organized as follows: An introduction, including a brief family history; a section on specific observances, divided into those between man and God and those dealing with man-to-man relationships. To this are appended the full text of Moses Nachmanides' ethical will, the full text of the Ten Commandments, and an annotated version of the Priestly Benediction, Numbers 6:24 – 26.

Philadelphia, September 16, 1955

A Father's Admonition

O Lord, open Thou my lips,
and let my mouth declare Thy praise.

Before a Jew begins to pray the *Amidah,* the silent prayer, he utters these words, so as to prepare himself for his task, so that no alien thoughts should enter his mind, so that all that comes from his mouth is pure and true and comes not only from his mouth, but from his heart as well, from the bottom of his soul.

I too want to begin this last will and testament—which is also a kind of prayer, a prayer for the next generation and the ones which come after, a prayer uttered for their sake, for their good counsel—with a preface.

Why do I leave this will? This is a question that would not have had to be asked a hundred years ago or more when it was common for a Jew to leave not only a will of property but a will of advice, an ethical will. A man should provide for the next generation materially—this is the duty of every father, his undeniable responsibility—but he must provide for them spiritually as well; he must seek to make their way in life easier by showing them where the path is to be found which will guide them through the forest of daily living where it is so easy to lose both body and soul. In setting down this will, then, I am but doing what countless Jews have done before me in days gone by, and what I hope will again be taken up as a sacred *mitzvah** by our generation.

Now the time has come for me to set down for you, dear children (and by "children" I include my daughters-in-law, my son-in-law, and my grandchildren), certain advice and rules of conduct which *I urge you and request you to accept* as a guide for your own lives. *Take a father's advice and counsel*—from a heart disturbed at the thought of parting from you at some future time, as a sea disturbed in the storm. My children, *listen to my rules of conduct,* neglecting none of my instructions. Set my advice before your eyes, and let it be your guide.

Thousands of years ago our forefathers stood at Mount Sinai and entered into a covenant with the Lord. God made that covenant not only with the generation which stood amid the thunder and lightening that day and received the Ten Commandments, but with every generation which was to come afterward.

How can we renew the covenant with God? By living according to the spirit and letter of the Torah, by observing the *mitzvos.* There are two divisions of *mitzvos* which have traditionally been made: the *mitzvos* between man and God, and the *mitzvos* between man and man. Let me write of them briefly in that order.

Mitzvos *Between Man and God*

Prayer

Prayer is to the soul what food is to the body. We cannot live without it, and if we try to, our souls become sick just as our bodies would become sick without food. To pray does not mean to ask *for something,* but to be *with Someone,* to spend a few minutes each day speakng with God, coming in contact with the noble ideals of the *Siddur* [prayerbook]: justice, righteousness, love of God, love of man, love of Torah. It should be a regular discipline in your lives and a source of daily guidance and strength.

*Divine precept; biblical commandment; meritorious deed.

Sabbath and Holidays

We cannot live as Jews without the Sabbath. The more I see it observed in the breach all about me, the more I am convinced of this fact. It is the source and wellspring of all Jewish values, the foundation of family life, the basis of the synagogue, the meaning for the rest of the days of the week. Of course, on the Sabbath you should not work, no matter what financial loss is incurred. Furthermore, you should not discuss business, nor even think of it. On the Sabbath ... we devote ourselves more to spiritual matters, to the synagogue, to prayer, to reading a book, taking a walk, spending time with the family.

The other holidays too, Yom Kippur, Rosh Hashanah, Pesach, Shavuot, and Succot should be strictly kept. These are the days of the year which give meaning to the rest of the days.

Kashrut [Dietary Rules]

Eating is something we have in common with the animals. Our religion endeavors to sanctify and ennoble, to raise the eating of food to a higher level. The Bible tells us to eat kosher food in order to be holy, which means to be a people set apart for a special task. We do not eat the blood of the meat, because blood is the source of life. The table is compared to the altar of old. Thus we should treat the table as a holy place.

Talmud Torah

The study of Torah is more important than all the other *mitzvos,* because it leads to the observance of the *mitzvos.* I want you, my children, not only to observe the Torah and to love the Torah but to understand the Torah. And this requires study. I do not speak now of the importance of giving your children, girls as well as boys, as good a Hebrew education as possible—this I know you will do—but of something more difficult, of studying Torah yourself. Despite the pressures of business and family matters, I urge you to set a fixed time for the study of Torah. You should hire a private teacher to come to your home or even to the office several hours a week so that you can engage in one of the most rewarding *mitzvos*—the study of Torah, for it is our life and the length of our days, and we should meditate in it day and night.

Mitzvos *Between Man and Man*

Shalom—Peace

"Be of the disciples of Aaron who love peace and pursue peace and draw people close to the Torah" (*Ethics of the Fathers* I, 12). Do not allow the coals of anger and contention and strife to be kindled within you, for they will consume and pervert your energies, make enemies out of friends, bring dissension into your home, and cause you to become bitter and unfriendly.

Pride

Many times the reason we do not get along with others is because of pride, because we are overly sensitive about ourselves, concerned only how the other person's words or actions affect us. We think that we and our petty problems are the center of the universe and have no interest or concern for others. Humility is the best of all good qualities. For this virtue Moses our teacher was praised, as it is said, "Now the man Moses was very meek" (Num. 12:3). If we are humble, then we realize that there are other people in the world besides ourselves. Even God, according to the Talmud, says "An arrogant man and I cannot live in the same world."

No matter how great your wealth, how powerful your position, live quietly, eat moderately, dress simply, speak gently, and conduct all your affairs with humility.

Justice

The word for justice in Hebrew is *tzedek*. It means to do what is right, what is straight, what is honest. And it applies most of all to our lives as businessmen, though of course it includes the rest of our lives as well. To be honest in business is not easy. There are many temptations, many opportunities each day to take advantage of the next fellow in an improper way, and there are many who follow this path. They think that because it seems to be a shortcut, it will get them where they want to go. But in the end it is diligence and hard work that pay in business, and a good name is worth more than money dishonestly gotten. Our sages tell us that the first question a man will be asked when he comes to the heavenly court for judgment is "Have you dealt honestly in your business?"

Charity

Another word for justice is *tzedakah,* which is the word we commonly use to mean charity. But how can the same word mean both justice and charity? What does this teach us? It teaches us that, to our forefathers and to us, giving charity is only doing what is just and right. We do not deserve any great praise if, because we have more, we give to those who have less. We are simply doing what is right and just. The possessions we own today were owned by someone else before we were born and will be owned by someone else after we are gone. We are only tenants, trustees, stewards of whatever we possess. Thus we must use our wealth with a sense of responsibility toward others.

I have endeavored to be charitable to all worthwhile causes; I am particularly proud of having had the Central Talmud Torah building erected during my presidency and the Bnei Jeshurun synagogue built during my presidency, of stimulating the establishment of the chair in Hebraic Studies at Temple University and establishing the permanent chair in Hebraic Studies at the University of Pennsylvania, of being one of the founders of the Yeshiva University Medical School, and of founding the Har Zion Midrasha — College of Jewish Studies and many others.

May you continue to observe the biblical law of tithe, which is to give at least ten percent of your income to charity, and may you also continue the Abraham M. and Rose Ellis Foundation which I established several years ago for the cause of charity.

Envy

If we are only stewards of the wealth we own, if our homes, our stocks, and our business belong to God as well as to us, then we must be grateful for what we have and not envy the property of others. My children, jealousy can destroy a man and envy can sometimes harm a person beyond repair. It can arouse within us hurtful feelings, the desire to overtake the other fellow no matter how it is done. And this we must by all means avoid. Only a sense of gratitude toward God for what we have can rid us of envy. "Who is rich?" ask the rabbis, "He who is satisfied with what he has" (*Ethics of the Fathers* IV, 1).

Love

The last *mitzvah* which I urge upon you, and the most difficult, is that of love, love between a man and his neighbor, between husband and wife, between parents and children, between brother and brother. The rabbis remark that "to love God truly, one must love man. And if anyone tells you that he loves God and does not love his fellowmen, you will know he is lying." You cannot love God and hate man. To love God means to love man, whether he be a Jew or non-Jew.

Now, my children, I have spoken to you with an open heart, sharing with you the fruits of my experience and the results of a long, long life. I have told you what I believe would be the best path for you to follow. I would like to address you individually, as Jacob did his children, and hope that I still shall. As is true with all fathers, I have received both pain and joy from you, my children. The joy was great and rich and gave me much happiness, but the pain was very unpleasant and brought me much sadness. Always there was your dear mother, like Rachel of old, patient and determined, to pacify me and give me patience. Of course, your mother's wise decisions in such cases were usually final.

I respectfully recommend to you, my children, that at least four times annually you reread this ethical will and try to follow its recommendations.

Mordecai Halpern

Mordecai Halpern (1885 – 1976) was born in Russia, in the city of Greiding, Podolia province, into a family acknowledged for its devotion to Judaism and charitable dispositions. The Jewish experiences of his childhood left a profound positive impression on his values, evident in his lifelong attachment to the religious and ethical precepts of Judaism, the principal themes in his will. In his advanced years, Mordecai Halpern pondered the writing of an ethical will for his family. To organize the array of values and concepts he wished to convey to them, he chose an alphabetical arrangement. His list included all the letters except X, Y, and Z. Excerpts of his privately published will are from each of the sections which he succeeded in completing before his death.

We of the old generation are bewildered by the new and strange world we find ourselves in. Think of the world in which some of us grew up, which seems so far away and long ago. It was simple and seemingly an innocent and idealistic world.

I recall in the days gone by people used to say "I will go to Philadelphia next week, God willing." When one asked his friend "How are you?" the usual answer was "Thank God." When one sneezed, it was customary to say "God bless you." Now we just say "Bless you." We are terribly afraid of seeming pious.

Religion is not a popular subject either. It used to be the very essence of Jewish existence. Now no phrase has become so current as the one "I am not religious."

The same indifferent attitude of our generation toward religious values is extended to moral values. People used to be judged by the kind of heart they have, by the moral values of their character. Now, they are estimated by their financial rating. One who has nothing is nothing.

We are witnesses to an unchecked drift away from our great heritage to the customs of the free world. No wonder the rate of mixed marriages is rising higher and higher. I am not worried about you, my children. You have memories and traditions from your childhood days, and these memories hold you somehow in check to a considerable degree. I am primarily concerned with *your* children, who are lacking the kind of a home you had, and I feel that it is my duty to do whatever I possibly can to prevent them from being caught in the dangerous drift of indifference and assimilation.

I have spent several sleepless nights brooding over what is to be done, and I came to the conclusion that the best thing I can do is to pass on to you in as simple and short as possible way some thoughts of our great heritage which I found helpful in my life, and what I learned from my experience in Jewish life for three-quarters of a century. I sincerely hope that it will clarify the Jewish way of life, so that it will not be regarded as a chain of an unwelcome fate, but as a proud invitation for a high calling.

In order to enable you to acquire easily any particular subject or topic, I have arranged it alphabetically.

Attitude

Attitudes are more important than facts. Any fact facing us is not half as important as our attitude toward that fact. And nothing yields to life so bountiful a harvest of good as a mental attitude that sees the best instead of the worst in everything.

Two people visit a rose garden. One comes back and says, "The bushes are full of thorns." The other returns and exclaims, "How beautiful the roses are!" Some people make life harder than necessary. They see only the worst instead of the best. They see the speck in the apple, the thorns in the rose bushes.

We often experience in life that our wishes are thwarted for our own good. We frequently hear that so and so met with a slight accident on his way to the airport and the necessitated delay saved his life. The Jewish optimistic attitude sees good arising out of apparent evil. Confidence in God and faith in the happy outcome of life will do more to lubricate the cracking machinery of our daily lives than anything else.

Belief

Belief and disbelief bear upon life and determine its course. All history is one solemn confirmation of the truth that in the same proportion that belief in God decreased, evil increased; and that in the same ratio that belief in God increased, evil diminished. There is no depth of wickedness to which people will not sink if thoroughly dispossessed of the belief in God (the Nazis have shown what man can do) and there is no height of elevation to which people will not aspire if thoroughly imbued with faith in God.

Belief, even though it cannot be proven, is not irrational. On the contrary, it supplies a more rational meaning to life which appears irrational without it. It gives some theory of life that brings order out of chaos.

Customs and Ceremonies

The ideas and ideals of a people may give it significance, but its group habits give it life. Naked ideas are frail things that often die upon being transplanted to a new climate. A minority people, fortified with concepts only, would have lost both its concepts and its life. A people bound by common law, ritual, and habitual practices, might save its law, its ideals, and even its life. We do not learn to love by theorizing about platonic love, but by loving; and we learn to do good not by talking about it, but by doing good. Judaism recognizes this truth and provides a network of ceremonies, symbols, and customs to keep ever bright the ideals we wish to preserve, to keep alive the memories of the past which fill us with pride in our great heritage. These symbols, customs, and ceremonies awaken in us our historic and group consciousness. They tie us with the generations of the past and unite us with the Jews all over the world. They bring the lesson of Judaism home to us in a striking and attractive form.

Children whose eyes have been filled and whose imaginations have been kindled by the colorful ceremonies in the home and by the beauty of the Sabbath and festival observances will carry them as their most precious treasure all their lives.

Discipline

We read in the book of *The Wisdom of Solomon,* 6 – 17: "The beginning of wisdom is the desire for discipline." These words are true to the art of life as they are true of the life of art. An artist must practice his art every day for many years. If he disregards his discipline, he loses fineness. So it is with the art of living. Judaism seems to have understood the average man and his struggle with his natural impulses and selfish inclination. To combat these, there are only the weapons of self-control, restraint, and discipline. But how can these weapons be obtained? Judaism says by inculcating the daily practice of good actions in conformity with the law.

At present one of the great needs of this age is the recognition of the Jewish conception of morality as law, and as long as self-conquest is noble, so long will these laws be worthwhile preserving.

Education

Jewish education is the golden hinge upon which our national and religious existence turns. It is the cornerstone in the maintenance of Jewish life.

Jewish education did not end with childhood or adolescence. It continued throughout life. The textbook was the Torah, and not only adults but also children were by and large well versed in it. The full significance of the value of Jewish learning among our people is best illustrated in a lullaby which was current in my hometown. Here is a part of it that I remember: "Sleep soundly, my darling, at night, and learn Torah by day. Then will you be a rabbi when I have grown gray."

Now, however, a large number of parents relieve themselves from the obligation to give their children a good Jewish education. They are disposed to believe that a secular education is good enough for their children. Let us see whether these parents are right! Our present system of secular education aims at smartness rather than at goodness. Our professional schools look at the careful training of the hand and the head, but leave the heart untouched. They produce practical and efficient people who are skillful and successful in their fields, but they neglect the training of character. Knowledge alone does not ensure character.

Jewish education does not signify the mere acquisition of information, but the enlightenment of the mind and the direction of the will toward truth, goodness, kindness, and unselfishness.

Faith

The word "faith" in the biblical language is *emunah,* which signifies an attitude of trust and confidence between man and God. To have *emunah* is to entrust oneself to God and to feel safe in that trust. To have *emunah* is to have faith that there are values worth being dedicated to and that there are ends worth being disciplined for.

The Jew had faith in God from the date he entered upon the scene of history. Our father Abraham, who began his career by breaking idols, was a searcher after truth, and his search after truth gave him the idea that the world and everything in it is the handiwork of God. "And he believed in God" the Torah tells us (Gen. 15:6).

God

Central in the teachings of Judaism is the idea of God, the Creator of heaven and earth. All the wisdom of man, Judaism maintains, is sheer and utter vanity unless it is accompanied by reverence and awareness of God. "Reverence of God is the beginning of wisdom" (Ps. 111:10). Our fathers were never in doubt as to the existence of God.

In our age, however, disbelief is in fashion, and there are quite a number of our younger generation who deny that God has any creative relation to the world. They claim that the universe is devoid of meaning and design. It is, they say, the mechanical result of the interaction of matter and energy. If order or harmony has happened at all, it has come as the result of an accident or chance. They challenge the believer to prove that there is a God who created the world.

There are some people who believe in the existence of God but they do not commit themselves to Him. They want God to do what they want. To do what He wants is too much for them. It would end their self-centeredness.

What about evil in the world? Can the God idea account for it? Well, I believe that God has some plan wherein so-called evil has a place. Because God does things for no reason that I can see is no proof that He does things for no reason at all. . . . I therefore believe in a good God, and although confused by the existence of evil, I suspend my judgment on this, knowing that my reasoning is too imperfect.

Happiness

The Torah advocates happiness. We are commanded in Deuteronomy 16:15, "Thou shalt be altogether joyful." We are told in the Talmud, *Shabbat* 30b, that "The *Shekhinah* [the Divine Presence] rests upon man not when he is depressed, but only when he is happy." (There are many more passages of this nature too numerous to quote.)

The Torah does not only advocate happiness, but indicates the path whereby real happiness can be attained. "And thou shalt rejoice, thou and thy son, and thy daughter, and thy man servant and maid servant, and thy stranger, and the fatherless, and the widow that are within thy gates" (Deut. 16:14).

"Who is rich? He who is happy with his lot" (*Ethics of the Fathers* IV, 1)." This is the only recipe for real happiness. It tells you that if it is happiness you seek, seek it in your home with your wife, your son, and your daughter; and that we must share our happiness with those who are less fortunate than we are.

Jewish Life

Jewish life is not merely a matter of performing traditional customs and ceremonies, as some people believe. It is a way of life. In one of the famous passages in Deuteronomy (32:47), "It is not a vain thing for you; it is your life," Moses describes Jewish life. It is not a theoretic and empty thing, he says. It means your very life. Unless the teachings and ideals of Judaism find expression in life they are not of much account.

The Jewish way of life has always been bound up with the idea of perpetuation. What the fathers received was valued as a prospective legacy to the children, and was meant to go down to them. We of this generation owe a debt to those who come after us to maintain our way of life. Moses was the greatest prophet. Yet what would his teachings have been worth if those who came after him had not kept it up?

The Talmud tells us that when God was about to give the Torah to Israel, He demanded some pledge that the Torah would be safe in their hands. The Israelites offered their ancestors, then the prophets, as pledges; but neither was accepted. Then they offered their children as their guarantee, and God accepted. History confirms that our forefathers faithfully complied with their promise. They preserved the Torah at the risk of their lives; and each generation, under much sacrifice, transmitted it to the next, down to our own generation.

It was this way of life that carried us through the struggle of all these centuries and helped us not only to survive, but also to live a meaningful and purposeful life.

The alphabetical presentation of Jewish values and concepts ends at this point.

Richard J. Israel

The following letter is not, strictly speaking, an ethical will. It was written by an expectant father as he waited outside the delivery room for the arrival of his as yet unborn child. It is included in this collection because it touches upon themes that many parents consider the most important in their lives. Rabbi Israel is Bnai Brith Hillel Director, New England Region.

To my (as yet) unborn child:

It is late. Though expectant fathers are supposed to be nervous, I am more restless than worried and wish you would already arrive.

Observing the children of friends, it is my impression that it may be some time before I will once again have the opportunity to address you in as much quiet as I have available this evening. Since talking to you at this time in the waiting room would merely raise questions in the nurse's mind about my potential competence as a stable parent, I shall commit this address to writing, to deliver it at some presently unknown and undesignated time.

I am full of expectations for you. Not about your sex. I don't have the least interest in whether you are a girl or a boy. Five or six children from now, if the law of average treats us shabbily, I might have some feelings about the question, but I don't now.

There are other matters that seem far more significant. It is, for example, very important to me that you be fun, not so that you should keep me amused, though I wouldn't mind that, but, more significantly, that you should be joyful. It appears that whatever you turn out to be, you are likely to be named after my father, who was an Isaac ("Yitzhak," from "laughter"), so that somehow your name will have to do with laughter or happiness, and that seems right. I do not commend earnestness to you as your chief virtue.

That does not mean that I don't want you to care about others. I want that very much. May you be able to be either kind or angry for others' sakes. You will know which is appropriate when the time comes. Even more, may you be willing from time to time to risk doing something that may turn out to be foolish, for the sake of a wise concern.

Tonight I am particularly conscious of our responsibilities to make the world a better place, since it is with mixed feelings of guilt and relief that I am now sitting in the hospital rather than driving to Montgomery, Alabama, with Bill Coffin and John Maguire (they drove off without me) in pursuit of what seems like a very important cause. (Someday, if you like, I'll tell you about them and what their adventure turned out to be.)

I write all this to warn both of us that I shall try not to live out my deficiencies through you but at the same time that I do not plan to abandon all goals and aspirations for you just because they happen to be mine, too. One goal that I think I shall not give up is that I want you to be clearly and irrevocably Jewish. I do not know if my way will be your way, but your way must be a real way, and a serious way. I won't give an inch on that one. It is perhaps a sign of our (or at least my) time that I am already taking a defensive posture on this issue. Perhaps for you being Jewish will be an easy and relaxed thing, not the struggle and effort it has been for me, but I don't feel compelled to wish you an easy time of it. Valuable things usually cost quite a bit. Perhaps part of your struggle will be with me.

I want you to be happy, caring, and Jewish. How am I going to get you to be any of them—ah, now the anxiety begins. I don't have the vaguest notion of what it means to be a parent or how one goes about the task. Doing what comes naturally is clearly no panacea. People have been doing that for years, and we can see what the results have been. But then what alternatives have I but to promise you that I will try hard and hope that you won't have to pay too much for my on-the-job training. If you try to forgive my mistakes, I'll try to forgive yours. We are both going to make them—lots.

But, alas, my noble sentiments are rapidly leaving me as I am slowly becoming engulfed by the desire to sleep and my impatience for you, or at least for Dr. Friedman, to appear with joyous tidings. The Almighty is clearly helping me to practice parenting even before your arrival. I am not sure that I am grateful for His concern in this area at this moment. In any event, my wishes for you and the Messiah are the same at this moment. May you both come speedily.

> With love of unknown and untested quality,
> Your expectant father

Epilogue

We have read a good number of ethical wills. As we have seen, one does not have to be a professional writer to compose an ethical will. One does not need big words or fancy quotes or a formal style. "Words that come from the heart enter the heart," and the recipients now treasure a last message that a parent bequeathed to them, even though it has spelling mistakes or errors in grammar. In the end those are not the things that matter the most.

We have seen wills in which people show great sensitivity and concern and we have seen some in which people express the resentments that they feel. But none was petty or mundane. Somehow when a person has only one more message left to give, he or she rises above the trivial and attains a level of significance.

One might have thought that an ethical will would be a morbid or a grim thing to write or to read but, as we see, it is not. An ethical will is a love letter from the beyond, often poignant and moving, but never morbid or grim. On the contrary, some of them bring a smile as well as a tear.

What is the purpose of an ethical will? Its meaning is perhaps best expressed in a comment that Rabbi Harold Kushner once made on a phrase that appears in the story of Jacob in the Bible. When Jacob meets his son Joseph after a separation of many years, when he sees that his child is still alive and that his child has children, he cries out: *"Amuta hapa'am,"* which literally means: "I will die this one time" (Gen. 46:30). It is a strange expression; does a person die more than one time?

Rabbi Kushner explains it this way. All human beings owe life one death. But if a person leaves behind no one who remembers his values and his character, if a person is forgotten as if he never was, that person dies a second death. This is what Jacob felt he was saved from when he saw his son and his son's sons. "I will die this one time," he said with relief and joy when he realized that his values would not die with him.

Nowadays every sophisticated person knows about insurance and estate planning and trusts. We all want to make sure that our property will be safeguarded after we are gone. The ethical wills in this collection were written by people who wanted to make sure that their values as well as their property would be safeguarded after they were gone. They were written by people who understood that you are not completely dead when you die if you leave behind people who understand what you stood for and who will carry on what you believed in.

Ethical wills are admittedly risky things to write. No one has a right to impose his values on his heirs, even from the grave. The end of life ought to be a time for making peace and for letting go, not a time for preaching, for judging, or for burdening. But an ethical will can be a love letter from the beyond, a summary of a spirit, to treasure and to live by afterward. If our children are willing to accept our material possessions from us, to use as they think best, then perhaps we have the right to bequeath our values and our goals to them too, in the hope that they will choose to accept them and make them their own.

Ken yehi ratzon.
So may it be.

—J.R.